BIB TRIVIA GAME

The Ultimate Bible Quiz Book to Test Your Knowledge and Improve Your Understanding of the Scriptures

Louis Richards

MONKEY
PUBLISHING

OUR HAND-PICKED
BOOK SELECTION FOR YOU.

LEARN
SOMETHING NEW
EVERYDAY.

ISBN: 9798405457932

As for me
and
my HOUSE
we shall serve
the LORD
~ Joshua 24:15 ~

"How did King Saul die?"

Do you know the answer to this question? The answer is that he killed himself on the battlefield, along with his armor bearer.

Now doesn't this make you wonder why?

This book is packed full of great fun trivia questions so you can test yourself or have a quiz with friends and family, but it also offers more. Alongside the answers you're also given Scripture references so you can find out more if your curiosity has been piqued. It's fun and educational!

The book is divided into 3 categories:

- Old Testament Trivia
- New Testament Trivia
- Extra-Biblical Trivia

Each quiz consists of five questions, perfect for keeping score, and offering you a chance to pause and delve deeper into the story behind the answers. The answers can be found in a separate section of the book, so you can test your own knowledge too.

We hope that you will find this book fun and enjoyable, an ideal way to bring The Bible to life and learn more about the word of God. It's suitable for all ages, for anyone who loves to learn and enjoys a quiz!

God Bless

CONTENT

DID YOU KNOW?

THE BIBLE CONTAINS 3,566,480 LETTERS.

Old Testament

TRIVIA

Quiz 1

1. On how many occasions was Saul left unharmed by David?
2. What did Saul attempt to offer to David, for his battle with Goliath?
3. Which judge conquered the Midianites, using an army of merely 300, wielding lights and horns?
4. What was the country of Moses' birth?
5. Which came first? The exodus of Egypt or the collapse of Jericho's walls.

Quiz 2

6. Were Joseph's brothers envious of his hat, his belt, his shoes, or his coat?
7. When David fled into the wilderness, did Saul stop pursuing him?
8. According to the book of Genesis, how many days did God spend creating?
9. Was David instantly accepted by the people when he was anointed as King over Israel?
10. What was the name of Abraham's wife?

Quiz 3

11. To which prominent authority did the southern kingdom surrender?
12. How was the size of David's army described?
13. What was Bathsheba's second child called?
14. On Mount Horeb, who did God make himself known to?
15. What happened to Joab after he had killed Absalom?

Quiz 4

16. Naaman, the leader of the army of Syria, was plagued by what illness?
17. Whom did God instruct Moses to send to explore the Promised Land?
18. Which nation was David's biggest foe while he was King?
19. According to the book of Genesis, what did God create first?
20. What name did God give to Abram?

Quiz 5

21. What is the second commandment?
22. Which Bible books hold a register of all the kings?
23. The enemy's temple had an idol next to the Ark. What happened to it?
24. How many years of famine did Joseph interpret Pharao's dreams as meaning?
25. What signal did God give to Noah, as a promise to never send an earth-destroying flood again?

Quiz 6

26. What new name did God give to Sarai?
27. What frightened the spies that were dispatched into Canaan?
28. Why were Joseph's brothers angry about his dreams?
29. What did God do to disseminate people over the world?
30. Name Isaac's two sons.

Quiz 7

31. Which of the Ten Commandment comes last?
32. What fate befell Bathsheba's first baby?
33. What object did God use to communicate with Moses in the desert?
34. Complete the sentence: "Two are better than one because they have a good return for their work: If one falls down, _____ _____ can help him up."
35. How did God punish Saul for defying his instruction?

Quiz 8

36. Which of Isaac's sons was his firstborn?
37. In what way did Esau supply for his family's needs?
38. Name the three sons of Noah. Shem, Ham, and Japheth.
39. How long did Jonah spend inside the large fish that swallowed him?
40. How many books make up the Old Testament?

Quiz 9

41. What miracle did God use Moses to perform, in order to rescue the Israelites fleeing from the Egyptians?
42. What was Saul known for?
43. How many of Saul's sons were killed in the battle in which he also died?
44. What happened to the Egyptians when they attempted to pursue the Israelites through the Red Sea?
45. While Moses was on Mount Sinai receiving the 10 commandments, what was Aaron busy making?

Quiz 10

46. What did Joseph do for Pharaoh's cupbearer and chief baker, who were imprisoned with him?
47. What command did God send to the Pharaoh through Moses?
48. When building the Tower of Babel, what were the people trying to achieve?
49. What was the name of the son of David who became a very wise king?
50. What place did Hagar and her son travel to?

Quiz 11

51. Which miraculous sign was first revealed to Moses by God?
52. What was the tenth plague that persuaded Pharaoh to free the slaves?
53. What did David order to happen to Uriah after Bathsheba became pregnant?
54. What explanation did Joseph's brothers give to his father for being gone?
55. Which person was instructed by God to leave Ur and go to Canaan?

Quiz 12

56. Which plague was the first to hit Egypt?
57. What vessel did Noah construct on God's command?
58. What gifts did God bestow on Solomon?
59. As Absalom approached, which city did David flee from?
60. In which way does God first reveal himself to Moses?

Quiz 13

61. What four words were written on the wall by a strange hand at King Belshazzar's banquet?
62. When Sarah was found barren, what did she suggest for Abram to do to become a father?
63. During creation, when was man made?
64. How many brothers did Joseph have?
65. Where in the Bible is the Fruit of the Spirit listed?

Quiz 14

66. Which man was David's close friend?
67. Where in the Bible would you find numerous wise quotes, such as, "a wise son makes his father glad, but a foolish son is a grief to his mother."
68. When the earth began, where did the humans live?
69. Which of Joseph's brothers offered to replace Benjamin to remain in Egypt?
70. Which person allowed the Israelites to go back home?

Quiz 15

71. There are seven sins listed in the Bible which are an abomination to God. Can you name them?
72. Jacob had a twin brother, what was his name?
73. Which person created a snake made of brass?
74. Which musical instrument was played by David, and which king did he play it for?
75. Who authored the Old Testament's first five books?

Quiz 16

76. Which devotee of God prayed thrice daily, and was cast into a lion's den by king Darius?
77. Before he became king, what occupation did David have?
78. Genesis is the first book in the Bible. What three words does it open with?
79. Who was the author of Psalm 90?
80. Which person was renamed Israel, and after what event did this happen?

Quiz 17

81. King Solomon received a visit from which well-known queen?
82. What structure was built for the Lord, by Solomon?
83. Which group of men came to Egypt due to the famine, and were recognized by Joseph?
84. Who took Moses' body for burial?
85. Where was Moses when the ten commandments were given to him?

Quiz 18

86. What was Moses' brother called?
87. Where was Saul going when he was blinded?
88. Where was Daniel taken after he broke the rules by praying to God?
89. Name Adam and Eve's three sons.
90. Which two birds did Noah send from the Ark?

Quiz 19

91. Which disaster was headed for Egypt but averted by Joseph?
92. Which person from Ur was instructed to move to an unknown country?
93. While the boy Samuel was asleep in the house of the Lord, how many times did God call to him?
94. Which strange land did David flee to?
95. Which person became the first King of Israel, anointed by Samuel?

Quiz 20

96. Can you give the names of three kings of Israel?
97. The Bible was written by several different people, but which one used the most words?
98. Where did the Israelites escape from out of slavery, assisted by Moses?
99. What was the first woman called?
100. What person did Abraham instruct to search for a wife for Isaac?

Quiz 21

101. What number of 'minor profits' are there?
102. After Joseph was bought by slave traders, where was he taken?
103. Who was Bathsheba married to?
104. What is the name of Abraham's second-born son?
105. Which of Laban's daughters did Jacob want to take as his wife?

Quiz 22

106. What is the collective name that the first five books of the Old Testament are known as?
107. After the fall in the Garden of Eden, whom was God calling when He asked, "Where art thou?"
108. What creature did Balaam ride on?
109. The whole book of Psalms was authored by David. True or False?
110. What was the name of the final king that Daniel served under?

Quiz 23

111. When God appeared to Abraham what was he instructed to use as an offering on mount Moriah?
112. Which Bible chapter has the most verses?
113. Complete the sentence, "The words of the wise heard in quiet are better than the shouting of a _____."
114. What was the name of Jacob's second son born from Rachel?
115. How many days did God spend on Creation?

Quiz 24

116. What grand act in Israel is King Solomon known for?
117. Who was the first man to be crowned King of the Hebrews?
118. What are the names of the two towns that were demolished by fire and brimstone?
119. What did Esau sell his birthright for?
120. Who did Jacob marry after being deceived by Laban?

121. When Noah built his Ark, how many of each species of animal did he take aboard?
122. On which mountain did Elijah and the prophets come together, so that he could show them that God is the only true god?
123. In which way was Saul killed?
124. How did Absalom die?
125. While Moses was talking to God, like which animal did he say the people of Israel may not be like?

Quiz 26

126. What was the second offense that David committed in the Bible?
127. What is the seventh of the Ten Commandments?
128. What were Joseph's brothers instructed to do on their next visit to Egypt?
129. Who was given a multi-colored coat by his father, eliciting the envy of his brothers?
130. Which weapon did Saul use while attempting to murder David?

Quiz 27

131. David's life was saved from Saul by his friend Jonathan. How did he do this?
132. In which chapters are the Ten Commandments outlined?
133. For what reason did the Pharaoh call Joseph out of prison?
134. What item was given to Joseph by his father Jacob, that caused envy amongst his brothers?
135. What assurance did God give to Abram when he showed him the sky full of stars?

136. What happened to Daniel when he refused to stop praying to God?
137. Which man murdered Absalom?
138. Following numerous years of living in the desert, which two Israelites were the only people able to enter the Promised Land?
139. Which man came back to Israel to rebuild Jerusalem's walls?
140. Who was the temptress who married Samson?

Quiz 29

141. Which prophet reprimanded David?
142. What will happen to you if you honor your father and mother?
143. What instruction comes ninth in the Ten Commandments?
144. Which group took Daniel to their land after defeating Judah?
145. Which city was defeated by Joshua and the Israelites after God broke down its walls?

Quiz 30

146. With which book does the Old Testament end?
147. Which judge battled the Philistines and made a Nazarite vow from when he was born?
148. Which commandment is fourth on the list?
149. Which Bible book commands you to "train up a child in the way he should go and when he is old he will not turn from it."
150. For how long did the Israelites have to eat unleavened bread, in the course of the Passover celebration?

Quiz 31

151. Who were the couple that God placed in the Garden of Eden?
152. The compilation of 150 songs and poems make up which Bible book?
153. Who governed Israel once Joshua passed away and the Promised Land was taken over by them?
154. Which other men were imprisoned with Joseph?
155. Who was the mother of Abraham's second-born son?

Quiz 32

156. Was Solomon devoted to God his entire life?
157. What happened to the staffs of the Pharaoh's men when they threw it down, after being faced by Moses?
158. In which way was Moses saved by his mother, when the Egyptian soldiers were looking for him?
159. What nationality was Goliath?
160. Which man murdered his brother?

Quiz 33

161. Of the Ten Commandments, which is the third? "You shall not take the name of the LORD your God in vain,"
162. Which King was recognized as being wise?
163. Which female judge headed Israel into victory?
164. Which of Isaac's two sons did he prefer?
165. What did Joseph instruct his brothers to do when they returned to Canaan?

Quiz 34

166. Which book did David have most authorship of?
167. Following the murder of an Egyptian, what did Moses do?
168. Which man called out the Israelites, when the Philistines arrived to attack them?
169. After beating the Amalekites, who did Saul imprison rather than kill, disobeying God's word?
170. For his battle with Goliath, what did David pick from the stream?

Quiz 35

171. Following Saul's death, who did Samuel ordain as king of Israel?
172. Which book does the Bible start with?
173. What daring thing did Esther risk with the king?
174. How were Ruth and Naomi connected to each other?
175. In Jericho, what did fifty fierce men offer to do for Elisha?

Quiz 36

176. What purpose did the tabernacle serve?
177. Which twins were said to have battled in their mother's womb?
178. Who was the remnant of Israel, as mentioned by Zephaniah?
179. When God did not answer Saul, who did Saul ask for guidance?
180. Who did David appoint to lead his army?

Quiz 37

181. Who told Jacob to take his father's blessing, since Isaac was on his deathbed and unable to see?
182. Which commandment is listed 8th?
183. To how many women was Solomon married?
184. Who is the first shepherd the Bible tells us about?
185. When Solomon's reign ended, what became of the kingdom?

Quiz 38

186. What did the rainbow signify after the flood?
187. Which Bible books tell the story of King David?
188. From which family's lineage did Paul come?
189. Whose words were, "I, myself, and my house, want to serve the lord."
190. In the Old Testament, which king was the richest and most honorable?

Quiz 39

191. What were the Babylonian names of the three friends who were with Daniel?
192. What did Jacob have to do before Laban allowed him to marry Rachel?
193. How often did Daniel pray to God?
194. By whom was Solomon persuaded to lose his faith in God?
195. Who ordained David as king, with only his family present?

Quiz 40

196. Which is the fifth commandment?
197. How many plagues descended on Egypt?
198. Who ascended Mount Nebo?
199. How many humans were aboard the ark?
200. What two things did God make come down from the sky when the Israelites were in the desert?

Quiz 41

201. Which of David's sons initiated an uprising against him?
202. Under what circumstances was Saul left unharmed by David for a second time?
203. What weapon did Samson use to kill a thousand Philistines?
204. David chose 5 stones for his battle with Goliath, but how many did he sling to kill the giant?
205. What did Esau do when he realized he had lost his birthright?

Quiz 42

206. Who was the first human created by God?
207. When David left Saul unharmed the first time, where were they?
208. To what status did Pharaoh promote Joseph?
209. For how long did the waters prevail while Noah and his family were in the ark?
210. Which king's dream was interpreted by Daniel?

Quiz 43

211. Jacob, who became known as Israel, had how many sons?
212. In what way did Joseph's brothers dispose of him?
213. Which event occurred first, Abel's murder, or the great flood?
214. What is the meaning of the word "Tekel"?
215. Is it correct that God commanded his people to teach their children his laws and to talk of them when they sit in their homes, when they walk around, when they lie down and when they rise; write them on the doorposts of their houses?

Quiz 44

216. What assurance did God give to Abram and Sarah, regardless of their age?
217. What introductory sentence comes before the Ten Commandments?
218. During the Creation, on which day were plants created?
219. When Saul didn't stop chasing David, where did David flee to?
220. What does the sixth commandment say?

Quiz 45

221. What did God instruct Moses to do before approaching the burning bush?
222. Who was Abram married to?
223. Which man was instructed to use his only son as an offering in the Bible?
224. When God instructed Samuel to anoint the next king, what did God say should not be his (Samuel's) prior consideration?
225. How did David kill Goliath, the Philistine soldier?

226. Which two plagues physically afflicted the Egyptians?
227. How did God provide food to the Israelites when they were living in the desert?
228. The High Priest could go into the Holiest Place, the innermost section of the temple where they kept the ark of the covenant box, only on one day of the year. Which day was this?
229. Which person is credited for writing the book of Lamentations?
230. What was the name of Samuel's grandson?

Quiz 47

231. Whom does God equate the Israelites with, according to the book of Isaiah?
232. In the Old Testament, what phrase described the people of Israel selected and set aside by God?
233. Where in the Bible is the wisdom of sages set out?
234. Who was Darius?
235. Who accused Joseph of attempted infidelity?

Quiz 48

236. When God asked, "Whom shall I send, and who will go for us?", what was Isaiah's answer?
237. Whom does Nahum mention when he had nearly finished his foretelling regarding Nineveh?
238. Who became a salt pillar after she turned back to see the fall of Sodom and Gomorrah?
239. When Israel's people went to Deborah for judgement, where was she stationed?
240. Joseph's youngest brother was who?

Quiz 49

241. What type of lady was worth more than rubies, as described in the Bible?
242. In which book in the Bible does this stanza appear: "To everything there is a season, and a time to every purpose under the heaven."
243. After killing his brother Abel, how was Cain disciplined?
244. In order to be made king, whom did Abimelech, Gideon's son, murder?
245. Samson was a very strong man, but what was the thing that would cost him his power?

Quiz 50

246. Who were Job's three comrades?
247. "Acquaint now thyself with him, and be at peace." Who does this sentence refer to?
248. Who was the father of Jesse?
249. Where did Micah hail from?
250. Once in the Promised Land, what did Joshua prohibit the Israelites from doing?)

Quiz 51

251. What are the missing words: "It is the glory of _____ to conceal a thing: but the honor of _____ is to search out a matter."
252. What kind of meal did Jacob give to his brother Esau in exchange for his birthright?
253. In which way were Shadrach, Meshach and Abednego released from the fire they were initially thrown into?
254. What similarity did Solomon draw between animals and humans?
255. Which book comes after Exodus?

256. After the death of Naomi's family, which daughter-in-law stayed with her?
257. At the beginning of Job 3, what event does Job lament?
258. A dead man became alive when he touched which prophet's bones?
259. According to Revelation, what did the fine linen in which the bride of the Lamb was clothed, represent?
260. Who was Phinehas?

Quiz 53

261. What was Othniel able to do when he was overcome by the Spirit of the Lord?
262. When Moses was hidden in a basket and placed in the Nile as a baby, who kept an eye on him?
263. Who did David have an affair with after he looked at her with desire, and afterwards had her husband killed?
264. How old did Methuselah grow, according to the Bible?
265. Which event occurred first, Jacob's demise, or Paul preaching on the Areopagus?

Quiz 54

266. When the northern kingdom of Israel fell to Assyria, who ruled the southern Kingdom?
267. Which words does Joel use to describe the Lord?
268. Which two people fashioned the idols of the calf of gold and the snake made out of bronze?
269. What did David tell Solomon to let the sons of Barzillai do?
270. What fate befell Ahab's 70 sons?

Quiz 55

271. When Haggai relayed a message from God, what did the people do?
272. How was Jacob related to Abraham?
273. Apart from Zechariah, which prophet went to Jerusalem to uplift the Israelites in completing the rebuild of the temple?
274. What were Joseph's sons' names?
275. Who is referred to as "the saint of the Lord" in Psalm 106?

Quiz 56

276. Which woman, who was a prostitute, was the prophet Hosea instructed to marry?
277. Which naturally fertile area did God pledge to the Israelites?
278. Which act causes the prophet Nathan to scold David?
279. Of what prominence was Belshazzar?
280. Which judge was exposed to the Philistines by his wife?

Quiz 57

281. Which evil queen wanted Elijah the prophet to be murdered?
282. When Moses did a survey of the people in the book of Numbers, which Israeli tribe had the least amount of people?
283. What musical instrument is a Kinnor, played by David?
284. Which prostitute hid Joshua's spies, when they came to conquer Jericho?
285. Daniel was thrown to the lions by which man?

Quiz 58

286. Give the names of three biblical women whose names start with "R".
287. On which day and month did they commemorate Passover?
288. After Solomon's rule ended, Israel divided into two kingdoms, what was the name of the Southern kingdom?
289. What happened to king Ahab after he died?
290. On his way to Jericho, who did Joshua come upon, who had his sword out?

Quiz 59

291. What memorable person was Michal?
292. Noah constructed the Ark using the wood from which tree?
293. When Elisha used Elijah's cloak to divide the Jordan, who was looking at him?
294. Which man fathered Methuselah?
295. After Absalom toppled David's throne, in which way did he show off?

Quiz 60

296. When Belshazzar held a feast, how many people did he invite?
297. What was Deborah's significance?
298. What does the word Israel mean?
299. Which Jewish celebration did the happenings in Esther result in?
300. What was Moses concealed in when he was an infant?

Quiz 61

301. After Moses had been found among the reeds, who became his nursemaid?
302. What was done to the animals that were used as offerings?
303. Who said that Sarah was his sister, instead of his wife?
304. In Jeremiah, what does God say Israel and Judah are like?
305. What is Jeremiah instructed to look for all through the streets of Jerusalem?

Quiz 62

306. While Elijah was concealed in the Kerith Ravine, what brought him food?
307. What act of worship conducted by the nations around the Israelites, did God particularly hate?
308. What did David have to do in order to marry Michal, king Saul's daughter?
309. What was Adam's third son called?
310. How many sons were born to David at Hebron?

Quiz 63

311. What did Rahab do to let the Israelites see her house when they invaded?
312. What does the author of Ecclesiastes proclaim to be?
313. Who was Solomon's successor to the throne?
314. Who was Zipporah married to?
315. What are the missing words: "He that spareth his rod _____ his son: but he that _____ him chasteneth him betimes."

Quiz 64

316. Which Egyptian handmaiden did Abraham have a child called Ishmael with?
317. "For the earth shall be filled with the knowledge of the glory of the LORD, as the waters cover the sea." Whose words are these?
318. In the book of Ezra, which priest built the altar of God?
319. Whom did God instruct regarding the valley of dry bones?
320. Which bird did Noah set free from the Ark first?

Quiz 65

321. Which nation endured more hardship than Sodom, according to the Bible?
322. Lebanon was famous for what kind of tree?
323. Who had to transport the ark of the covenant while the Israelites roamed the desert?
324. The Israelite elders or leaders were stationed in which place?
325. Which queen was the wife of Ahab, and a worshipper of Baal?

Quiz 66

326. In Ezekiel, which trio does God describe as exemplars of "righteousness"?
327. Who is the oldest person in the Bible?
328. According to Leviticus, what is the most important standard for staying in the Israelite camp?
329. After Abel's murder, where did Cain flee to?
330. Which king descended from the Son of Ruth?

331. Who was Ahasueros?
332. Which 3 things did Gideon use as weapons to conquer the Midianites?
333. Which person told the sun and moon to stop moving?
334. In which Psalm is the verse: "The Lord is my Shepherd I shall not want"?
335. What vocation did Zerubbabel have?

Quiz 68

336. When Jericho's walls were struck down, who bore the horns that were blown?
337. What was Moses' wife's name?
338. What did David do after the death of his baby with Bathsheba?
339. Which book comes before Daniel, and which book follows it?
340. Which son of David tried to overthrow him when he was very old?

Quiz 69

341. In Proverbs, what is a quarrelsome wife said to be like?
342. Who was the mother of Samuel, who vowed to God that she would devote her son to him?
343. Which prophet had a donkey that could speak?
344. Who is promised deliverance, according to the book of Obadiah?
345. What number of offspring did Noah have?

346. From when to when does the Old Testament report?
347. What was Lot's relation to Abraham?
348. What was the name of Ruth's husband?
349. In Nehemiah, what is the feast called that is celebrated in the seventh month?
350. Which person advised Belshazzar that Daniel was able to see what was written on the wall?

Quiz 71

351. Which event occurred first, Enoch's rapture, or the ascension of Elia?
352. After he was tested, how many more years did Job live?
353. Once Moses murdered the Egyptian, where did he flee to?
354. Which Persian queen was an Israelite who used her power to shield the Jewish people?
355. Which man was married to Abigail?

Quiz 72

356. Is Horeb a village or a mountain?
357. What were Abraham's brothers called?
358. What was Elisha's role in the Bible?
359. When he discovered that his brothers wanted to murder Joseph, who convinced them not to?
360. What did Hezekia's son Menasseh, become?

Quiz 73

361. What did Rahab do for a living?
362. Which man accompanied Paul when he first went out to preach?
363. What caused Cain to murder his brother Abel?
364. What age did Enoch reach?
365. How many chapters long is the book of Philemon?

Quiz 74

366. Who released a dove to go and search for dry land?
367. Who ruled Israel for the longest period of time?
368. Can you give the names of three prophets?
369. Which book in the Bible comes after John?
370. What topic is most evidently covered in Micah?

Quiz 75

371. When Judah was assaulted, how did the people of Edom react?
372. What work did Shelah's sons, Judah's grandsons, do for the king?
373. Who was the father of Ham, and what were the names of his brothers?
374. Which king could tell the time by use of a sundial?
375. Who was David married to first?

Quiz 76

376. What were Amram and Jochebed known for?
377. "Bread of deceit is _____ to a man; but afterwards his mouth shall be filled with _____." What words fill the gaps?
378. Which Israeli king was known to be wise?
379. Who was the son of Seth?
380. In which way was Abimelech morbidly mutilated?

Quiz 77

381. For what did David prepare a place in Jerusalem?
382. What is the place called where Jacob had a battle with God?
383. In what way was Daniel, the Jewish prophet, delivered to Babylon?
384. Who famously authored the following: "The Lord is my Shepherd, I shall not want"?
385. In order to settle in the Promised Land, how many kings were conquered by the Israelites?

Quiz 78

386. In Proverbs, how does Jaketh's son Agur refer to himself?
387. What do the words Jahweh-Schammah translate to in English?
388. To whom did God say the following: "if thou wilt walk in my ways, to keep my statutes and my commandments, as thy father David did walk, then I will lengthen thy days."?
389. What was the name of Jacob's first-born son?
390. On God's orders, which city was demolished by the Israelites, by going around it seven times whilst making a huge noise with their horns?

Quiz 79

391. Which woman did Jacob have to work seven years for, before her father allowed him to marry her?
392. What vow did David make to his wife Batsheba?
393. What does the Godly title El Shaddai translates to in English?
394. Which person did David instruct Ishbosheth, son of Saul, to bring to him?
395. What was Ruth's sister-in-law called?

Quiz 80

396. At what age was Samuel sent to live in the temple by his mother?
397. When Saul first encountered David, what did he do?
398. Which person said this, and to whom? "... the half was not told me. Your wisdom and prosperity surpass the report that I heard.".
399. Why did Daniel hesitate to explain to the king what his dream meant?
400. After king Zedekiah revolted, how did the king of Babylon punish him?

Quiz 81

401. When Rachel went away with Jacob, what did she take from Laban, her father?
402. Who was Jacob tricked into marrying, instead of her younger sister?
403. Between Paul, David and Hosea, who was one of God's prophets?
404. Of the two people jailed with him, whose dream was correctly interpreted by Joseph, saying he would be given his job back?
405. Who does this verse speak of: "He was unto me as a bear lying in wait, and as a lion in secret places."?

406. What did the Israelites do, causing God to punish them to roam through the desert for forty years before they were allowed to enter the Promised Land?
407. Which part of Adam's body was Eve fashioned from?
408. Which prophet from the Old Testament was around during king Josiah's rule?
409. Give the names of three soldiers spoken about in the bible.
410. Who decided where the Israelites had to worship God, in the Promised Land?

Quiz 83

411. What was the name of Joab's mother?
412. When Job's children were killed, where were they all busy eating and drinking?
413. The descendants of the people who went into the Promised Land prayed to two gods. Who were they?
414. Moses destroyed the stone tablets that the Ten Commandments were written on at Mount Sinai. Why did he do this?
415. Who was saved by the Israelites when they invaded Jericho?

Quiz 84

416. What was wrong with Mephiboseth?
417. Ahab desired to own the vineyard of Naboth, how did he get it in the end?
418. What happened to cause Israel to split into two kingdoms?
419. What made Jericho's people fear the Israelites?
420. Which two people did God have the first covenant with?

421. How does this sentence end: "Who so trusteth in the LORD, ..."?
422. Where in the Bible is the story of Haman told?
423. In Amos' time, which person was the priest of Bethel?
424. How does the prophet Micah identify God - He is "the God of _____"?
425. In which book is the story of David and Goliath found?

Quiz 86

426. What does the name of Loruhamah, daughter of Hosea, mean?
427. Who was Joshua's father?
428. Which word appears last in the Old Testament?
429. What was Moses instructed to do prior to his death, in a vision from God?
430. What should a man devote the first year of marriage to, according to a message from God to the Israelites?

Quiz 87

431. What four types of terminators did God vow to set down on the Israelites?
432. What was to be done to the tithes given to God by the Israelites?
433. In which way was Sisera, the ruler of the king of Canaan's forces, killed by Jael?
434. Who was this said to?
435. Even in death Saul and Jonathan were not split, they were faster than ____, and more powerful than ____. What are the missing words?

Quiz 88

436. What did Job usually do after a banquet?
437. On the temple that Solomon constructed, what were the names of the two columns?
438. What was the name of the woman Abraham's servant brought to be Isaac's wife?
439. The religious details of life were tended to by which Israeli tribe?
440. What did Job's friends do to cause God to rebuke them?

Quiz 89

441. What did Adonijah do, that caused his younger brother Solomon to murder him?
442. How was Eglon, the king of Moab, pictured in the Bible?
443. What was Ezra's occupation in the Israelite community?
444. Which words were on the holy crown of the high priest?
445. Which person often stood in for Moses during speeches, because Moses was "slow of speech and slow of tongue"?

Bonus Quiz

446. In which bible book are apples first spoken of?
447. In the Old Testament, how are sins atoned for?
448. In which way was Uriah's death orchestrated?

Old Testament

Testament

TRIVIA

Answers

Answer – Quiz 1

1. Twice
2. His armor (1 Sam.17:38)
3. Gideon Judges (Chapters 7-9)
4. Egypt (Exodus chapter 2)
5. Exodus (Exodus 14 and Joshua 6)

Answer – Quiz 2

6. His coat (Genesis 37:3)
7. No (1 Samuel 23:13-15; 26:2)
8. Six days (Genesis 1:31)
9. Yes (2 Samuel 5:3)
10. At first it was Sarai, but God renamed her Sarah (Gen.17:15).

Answer – Quiz 3

11. The Southern Kingdom of Israel, known as Judah, fell to King Nebuchadnezzar of the Babylonians in 587 B.C. (2 Kings 24:12)
12. So many soldiers came to help David, their number was "like an army of God". (1 Chronicles 12:22)
13. Solomon (2 Samuel 12:24) Her first child died at the age of 7 days (2Sa 12:18).
14. Moses. (Exodus 3:1-6).
15. He was demoted from being commander. (2 Samuel 19:13).

Answer – Quiz 4

16. Leprosy. (2 Kings 5:1)
17. Twelve men - one chief man from each tribe (Numbers 13:2)
18. The Philistines. (2 Samuel Chapters 5, 8, 21, 23; 1 Chronicles Chapters 14 & 18).
19. The heavens and the earth (Genesis 1:1)
20. Abraham (Genesis 17:5) meaning "father of many nations".

Answer – Quiz 5

21. "You shall not make for yourself a carved image, or any likeness of anything that is in heaven above, or that is in the earth beneath, or that is in the water under the earth. You shall not bow down to them or serve them" (Exodus 20:4-5)
22. 1st & 2nd Kings, and 1st & 2nd Chronicles.
23. The idol Dagon fell face downward on the ground before the ark of the Lord and broke apart (1 Samuel 5:4)
24. Seven years of famine came after 7 good years (Genesis 41:1-36)
25. The rainbow (Genesis 9:9-17).

Answer – Quiz 6

26. Sarah (Genesis 17:15)
27. The giant soldiers of the enemy (Numbers 13:32-33).
28. Joseph's dreams indicated his brothers' submissiveness to him. (Genesis 37:5-11).
29. He confused their language (Genesis 11:6-9).
30. Esau and Jacob (Genesis 25:25).

Answer – Quiz 7

31. "You shall not covet" (Exodus 20:17)
32. He died at the age of seven days (2Sa 12:18).
33. A burning bush (Exodus 3:1-2)
34. His fellow (Ecclesiastes 4:9-10).
35. The Spirit of the Lord departed from Saul, and a harmful spirit from the Lord tormented him.(1 Samuel 16:14) Ultimately he committed suicide after having been wounded in battle (1 Samuel 31:4)

Answer – Quiz 8

36. Esau (Genesis 25:25)
37. He hunted (Gen.25:27)
38. Genesis 5:32.
39. Three days and three nights (Jonah 1:17).
40. 39 Books

Answer – Quiz 9

41. Moses stretched his hand over the sea, the waters parted and they went through on dry land. (Exodus 14:21-22)
42. Persecuting Christians (Acts 9:1-2)
43. Three: Jonathan, Abinadab and Malchi-shua, (1 Samuel 31:2)
44. The sea covered them and they drowned (Exodus 14:23-28)
45. A golden calf (Exodus 32:1-4)

Answer – Quiz 10

46. He interpreted their dreams for them (Genesis chapter 40)
47. "Let my people go, that they may hold a feast to me in the wilderness." (Exodus 5:5:1)
48. The were trying to prevent themselves from being "dispersed over the face of the whole earth." (Genesis 11:4)
49. Solomon (2 Samuel 5:14; 1 King 4:29-34)
50. To the wilderness of Beersheba (Genesis 21:14)

Answer – Quiz 11

51. Moses' staff turned into a serpent (Exodus 7:9-10)
52. The firstborn of every Egyptian family died in the same night (Exodus 12:29)
53. King David first tried to let him sleep with his wife, but he did not. Then he ordered that Uriah be set in the forefront of the hottest battle, where he died (2 Samuel 11:1-17)
54. That wild animals had devoured him (Genesis 37:31-33)
55. Abram (Genesis 11:31)

Answer – Quiz 12

56. Water turned into blood (Exodus 7:17-20)
57. The ark (Genesis 6:13-14)
58. Wisdom and understanding (1 Kings 4:29)
59. Jerusalem (2 Samuel 15:8, 14, 37)
60. He spoke to Moses from a burning bush (Exodus 3:1-4)

Answer – Quiz 13

61. "MENE, MENE, TEKEL, UPHARSIN. (Daniel 5:25)
62. Sarah took Hagar her maid the Egyptian, after Abram had dwelt ten years in the land of Canaan, and gave her to her husband Abram to be his wife. (Genesis 16:3)
63. On the sixth day (Gen.1:27, 31)
64. Eleven brothers (Long history through Genesis) (Genesis 5:22)
65. Galatians 5:22-23.

Answer – Quiz 14

66. Jonathan (1 Samuel 19:1-6)
67. The book of Proverbs
68. In the garden of Eden (Genesis 2:8)
69. Judah (Genesis 44:12-18, 32)
70. The Persian king, Cyrus (2 Chronicles 36:22-23)

Answer – Quiz 15

71. Haughty eyes, a lying tongue, and hands that shed innocent blood, a heart that devises wicked plans, feet that make haste to run to evil, a false witness who breathes out lies, and one who sows discord among brothers (Proverbs 6:16-19).
72. Esau (Genesis 25:25-26)
73. Moses (Numbers 21:9)
74. David played the lyre for Saul (1 Samuel 16:23)
75. Moses

Answer – Quiz 16

76. Daniel (Daniel 6:16)
77. Shepherd. (1 Samuel 16:11, 19; 17:15)
78. In the beginning (Genesis 1:1)
79. Moses (Ps. 90:1)
80. Jacob, renamed by God, appearing in the form of "a man" who wrestled with him during the night. (Genesis 32:24-30)

Answer – Quiz 17

81. The queen of Sheba (1 Kings 10:1)
82. The house of the Lord (1 King 6:1)
83. Joseph's brothers (Genesis 42:7)
84. Nobody. The Bible is silent about what happened to Moses' body (Deuteronomy 34:7)
85. On Mount Sinai (Exodus 19:2, 20; 20:1-17)

Answer – Quiz 18

86. Aaron (Exodus 4:14)
87. Damascus (Acts 9:2-8)
88. Cast into the lions' den (Daniel 6:16)
89. Cain, Abel and Seth (Genesis 4:1, 25);
90. A dove and a raven (Genesis 8:7-8)

Answer – Quiz 19

91. Famine (Genesis 41:54; 47:20)
92. Abram (Genesis 12:1)
93. Four times (1 Samuel 3:1-10)
94. Rama (1 Samuel 20:1)
95. Saul (1 Samuel 15:1)

Answer – Quiz 20

96. Saul (1 Samuel 15:1; David (1 Samuel 16:1, 13) and Solomon (1 Kings 1:39)
97. Moses (the 1st 5 books of the Bible)
98. Egypt (Book of Exodus Chapters 1-14)
99. Eve (Genesis 3:20)
100. His eldest servant (Genesis 24:2-4)

Answer – Quiz 21

101. Twelve: The last 12 books in the Old Testament, from Hosea to Malachi.
102. To Egypt (Genesis 37:28)
103. Uriah the Hittite (2 Samuel 11:3)
104. Isaac (Genesis 16:1-15; 17:20)
105. Rachel (Genesis 29:18)

Answer – Quiz 22

106. The Pentateuch
107. Adam and Eve (Genesis 3:8-9)
108. A donkey (Numbers 22:21)
109. False
110. Darius (Daniel 11:4)

Answer – Quiz 23

111. His only son, Isaac (Genesis 22:2)
112. Psalm 119
113. Ruler among fools (Ecclesiastes 9:17)
114. Benjamin (Genesis 35:24)
115. Six days (Genesis 1:31)

Answer – Quiz 24

116. He built a house for the Lord (1 Kings 6:1)
117. Saul (1 Samuel 15:1)
118. Sodom and Gomorrah (Genesis 19:24)
119. Bread and a pot of lentils (Genesis 25:29-34)
120. Leah (Genesis 29:23)

Answer – Quiz 25

121. Seven pairs of male and female of all clean animals and birds, and one pair of each of the unclean animals (Genesis 7:2-3, 8-9)
122. Mount Carmel (1 Kings 18:19)
123. He committed suicide by falling onto his own sword (1 Chronicles 10:4)
124. His head was caught in an overhead tree, where Joab and his men killed him (2 Samuel 18:9-15)
125. Like sheep (Numbers 27:17)

Answer – Quiz 26

126. He numbered the people (1 Chronicles 21:1-2)
127. "You shall not commit adultery." (Exodus 20:14)
128. To bring their youngest brother, Benjamin, to him in Egypt (Genesis 42:15-16)
129. Joseph (Genesis 37:3)
130. A spear (1 Samuel 18:11)

Answer – Quiz 27

131. Warned David about Saul's intention to kill him and worked peace between them (1 Samuel 19:2-6)
132. Exodus 20 and Deuteronomy 5
133. To interpret Pharaoh's dreams (Genesis 41:15)
134. A coat of many colours. (Genesis 37:3)
135. "So shall your offspring be." (Genesis 15:5)

Answer – Quiz 28

136. He was thrown into a den of lions (Daniel 6:6-16)
137. Joab (2 Samuel 18:14)
138. Joshua and Caleb (Numbers 14:26-30)
139. Nehemiah (Nehemiah 2:17; Chapter 3)
140. Delilah (Judges 16:4)

Answer – Quiz 29

141. Nathan (2 Samuel 12:1-12)
142. Your days will be long in the land that the LORD your God is giving you. (Exodus 20:12)
143. "You shall not steal." (Exodus 20:15)
144. Babylonians (Daniel 1:1-6)
145. Jericho (Joshua 6:3-20; Hebrews 11:30)

Answer – Quiz 30

146. Malachi
147. Samson (Judges chapters 13-16)
148. To keep the Sabbath (Exodus 20:8)
149. Proverbs 22:6
150. Seven days (Exodus 12:15)

Answer – Quiz 31

151. Adam and Eve (Genesis 2:8)
152. Psalms
153. The Judges
154. The Pharaoh's cupbearer and chief baker (Genesis 40:1-2)
155. Sarah (Genesis 16:15 & 21:3)

Answer – Quiz 32

156. No. when Solomon was old his wives turned away his heart after other gods, and his heart was not wholly true to the Lord his God, (1 King 11:4)
157. They turned into serpents, but Aaron staff, that had also turned into a serpent, swallowed them up (Exodus 7:10-12).
158. She hid him in a basket, where he was found by the pharaoh's daughter (Exodus 2:1-10)
159. Philistine (1 Samuel 17:23)
160. Cain (Genesis 4:8)

Answer – Quiz 33

161. Exodus 20:7
162. Solomon (1 Kings 10:23)
163. Deborah (Judges 4:4)
164. Esau (Genesis 25:8)
165. Genesis 43:3

Answer – Quiz 34

166. Psalms
167. He fled to Midian (Exodus 2:15)
168. Goliath (1 Samuel 17:1-8)
169. Agag (1 Samuel 15:8-9)
170. 5 smooth stones (1 Samuel 17:40)

Answer – Quiz 35

171. David (1 Samuel 16:13)
172. Genesis
173. She went to the king, which was then against the law (Esther 4:16)
174. Ruth was Naomi's daughter-in-law. (Ruth 1:22)
175. To go and search for Elijah (2 Kings 2:16)

Answer – Quiz 36

176. A sanctuary for God, that he may dwell among his people (Exodus 25:8)
177. Esau and Jacob (Genesis 25:22, 26)
178. House of Judah (Zephaniah 2:7)
179. The late prophet Samuel (1 Samuel 28:7-11)
180. Joab (2 Samuel 19:13)

Answer – Quiz 37

181. His mother Rebekah (Genesis 27:6-10)
182. "You shall not steal." (Exodus 20:15)
183. 700 (1 Kings 11:3)
184. Abel (Genesis 4:2)
185. Rehoboham became king (1 Kings 12:1-6).

Answer – Quiz 38

186. Never again shall all flesh be cut off by the waters of the flood, and never again shall there be a flood to destroy the earth." (Genesis 9:11)
187. 1st & 2nd Samuel
188. Posterity of Israel, tribe of Benjamin. (Romans 11:1)
189. Joshua (Joshua 24:2-15)
190. Solomon (1 Kings 10:23)

Answer – Quiz 39

191. Shadrach, Meshach and Abednego (Daniel 1:7)
192. Work a further 7 years (Genesis 29:30)
193. Three times per day (Daniel 6:11)
194. By his wives (1 Kings 11:4)
195. Samuel (1 Samuel 16:13)

Answer – Quiz 40

196. "Honor your father and your mother,…" (Exodus 20:12)
197. Ten (Exodus chapters 7-13)
198. Moses (Deuteronomy 34:1
199. Eight (Genesis 7:13)
200. Quail and Manna (Exodus 16:13, 31)

Answer – Quiz 41

201. Absalom (2 Samuel 15:10)
202. While Saul was sleeping among his soldiers, David could have killed him with his own spear. (1 Samuel 26:3-12)
203. Jawbone of a donkey (Judges 15:15)
204. Only one (1 Samuel 17:49)
205. He threatened to kill Jacob as soon as their father would die (Genesis 27:41)

Answer – Quiz 42

206. Adam (Genesis 1:27)
207. In a cave (1 Samuel 24:1-6)
208. Vice-pharaoh (Genesis 41:41-45)
209. 150 days (Genesis 7:24)
210. Nebuchadnezzar's (Daniel 2)

Answer – Quiz 43

211. Twelve (Genesis 35:12)
212. They sold him to Ishmaelite traders (Genesis 37:28)
213. Abel's murder (Genesis 4:8)
214. "you have been weighed in the balances and found wanting;" (Daniel 5:27)
215. Yes. (Deuteronomy 6:6-9; 11:18-20)

Answer – Quiz 44

216. That they would have a child the next year (Genesis 18:10-11)
217. "I am the LORD your God, who brought you out of the land of Egypt, out of the house of slavery." (Exodus 20:2)
218. On the 3rd day (Genesis 1:11-12)
219. He went to Achish the king of Gath. (1 Samuel 21:10)
220. "You shall not murder." (Exodus 20:13)

Answer – Quiz 45

221. To take off his shoes (Exodus 3:5)
222. Sarai (Genesis 11:29)
223. Abraham (Genesis 22:2)
224. His appearance or his stature (1 Samuel 16:7)
225. With a stone from his slingshot (1 Samuel 17:40-50)

Answer – Quiz 46

226. Gnats and boils. (Exodus 8:17; 9:10)
227. Bread rained down from heaven and quail came down to them (Exodus 16:4,13)
228. On the day of atonement (Exodus 30:10; Leviticus 16:2)
229. Jeremiah (Lamentations 1:1)
230. Heman (1 Chronicles 6:33)

Answer – Quiz 47

231. Sodom and Gomorra (Isaia 1:9-10)
232. A peculiar treasure (Exodus 19:5; Psalm 135:4)
233. In Proverbs
234. King of Persia (Ezra 4:5)
235. Potiphar's wife (Genesis 39:11-20)

Answer – Quiz 48

236. "Here am I; send me." (Isaia 6:8)
237. The king of Assyria. (Nahum 3:18)
238. Lot's wife (Genesis 19:26)
239. Under the palm tree of Deborah (Judges 4:5)
240. Benjamin (Genesis 44:12)

Answer – Quiz 49

241. A virtuous woman (Proverbs 31:10)
242. Ecclesiastes 3:1
243. God spoke his punishment in '(Genesis 4:11-12).
244. Seventy of his brothers (Judges 9:56)
245. Cutting of his hair (Judges 16:19-21)

Answer – Quiz 50

246. Eliphaz the Temanite, and Bildad the Shuhite, and Zophar the Naamathite (Job 2:11)
247. To God (Job 22:17, 21)
248. Obed (Ruth 4:22)
249. Moresheth (Mica 1:1)
250. Not make mention of the name of their gods, nor cause anyone to swear by them; and shall not serve them nor bow down to them (Joshua 23:7)

Answer – Quiz 51

251. God; kings. (Proverbs 25:2)
252. A brew of lentils (Genesis 25:34).
253. King Nebuchadnezzar called them to come out (Daniel 3:26)
254. They all die (Ecclesiastes 3:19)
255. Leviticus

Answer – Quiz 52

256. Ruth (Ruth 1:14)
257. His birth (Job3:3)
258. Elisha's (2 Kings 13:21)
259. The righteous deeds of the saints (Revelation 19:8)
260. A priest, the son of Elehazer (Joshua 22:30)

Answer – Quiz 53

261. He was able to deliver Israel from Cushan-rishathaim, king of Mesopotamia. (Judges 3:8-10)
262. His sister (Exodus 2:4)
263. Bathsheba (2 Samuel 11:2-5)
264. 969 years (Genesis 5:27)
265. Jacob's demise (Genesis 49:33; Hebrews 11:21; Acts 17:19-22)

Answer – Quiz 54

266. Hezekia (2 Kings 18:1)
267. Gracious and merciful (Joel 2:13)
268. Respectively: Aaron (Exodus 32:2-4) and Moses (Numbers 21:9)
269. "Deal loyally with the sons of Barzillai the Gileadite, and let them be among those who eat at your table," (1 King 2:7)
270. They were slaughtered and their heads put in a basket (2 Kings 10:7)

Answer – Quiz 55

271. The Jews built and prospered through the prophesying of Haggai the prophet (Ezra 6:14)
272. Jacob was Abraham's grandson (Genesis 21:3; 25:26)
273. Haggai (Ezra 6:14)
274. Manasseh & Ephraim (Genesis 46:20)
275. Aaron (Psalm 106:16)

Answer – Quiz 56

276. Gomer (Hosea 1:3)
277. Canaan (Exodus 3:8)
278. His affair with Bathsheba, wife of Uriah (2 Samuel 12:1-7)
279. A king (Daniel 5:1)
280. Samson (Judges 16:18-21)

Answer – Quiz 57

281. Jezebel (1 Kings 19:2)
282. Manasseh (Numbers 1:1-44)
283. A harp (1 Samuel 16:23)
284. Rahab (Joshua 2:1)
285. King Darius (Daniel 6:9, 16)

Answer – Quiz 58

286. Ruth (Ruth 1:4); Rahab (Joshua 2:1); Rebecca (Romans 9:10)
287. The fourteenth day of the first month (Leviticus 23:5)
288. Judah (Joshua 18:5)
289. He was buried in Samaria (1 Kings 22:37)
290. The LORD, in his capacity of Commander of the army of the Lord (Joshua 5:13-14; 6:1-2)

Answer – Quiz 59

291. Younger daughter of king Saul (1 Samuel 14:49)
292. Gopher trees (Genesis 6:14)
293. Fifty men of the sons of the prophets (2 Kings 2:7)
294. Enoch (Genesis 5:21)
295. They pitched a tent for Absalom on the top of the house, and Absalom went in to his father's concubines in the sight of all Israel. (2 Samuel 16:22)

Answer – Quiz 60

296. A thousand (Daniel 5:1)
297. She was both a prophetess and a judge (Judges 4:4)
298. Composed of three Hebrew words: ISH, means "man"; RA means important/, weighty/, heavy; EL is the Name Elohîm abbreviated. ISH-RA-EL wants to convey "MAN who is IMPORTANT to (or HAS WEIGHT with) EL (Elhohîm, God) (Genesis 32:28)
299. Purim (Esther 9:26-28)
300. A basket (Exodus2:3-10)

Answer – Quiz 61

301. His own mother (Exodus 2:7-8)
302. Burnt outside the camp. (Leviticus 4:12. 21)
303. Abraham (Genesis 20:2)
304. Like treacherous sisters (Jeremiah 3:6-10)
305. See if you can find a man, one who does justice and seeks truth, (Jeremiah 5:1)

Answer – Quiz 62

306. Ravens (1 Kings 17:4-6)
307. Offering their sons and daughters to Molech (Jeremiah 32:35)
308. 'The king desires no bride-price except a hundred foreskins of the Philistines, (1 Samuel 18:25-27)
309. Seth (Genesis 4:25)
310. Six (2 Samuel 3:2-5)

Answer – Quiz 63

311. Tie a red/scarlet cord to her window (Joshua 2:18)
312. Preacher, son of David (Ecclesiastes 1:1)
313. Rehoboam (1 King 11:43)
314. Moses (Exodus 2:21)
315. Hates, loves (Proverbs 13:24)

Answer – Quiz 64

316. Hagar (Genesis 16:15)
317. Habakkuk (Habakkuk 2:14)
318. Joshua (Ezra 3:2)
319. Ezekiel (Ezekiel 7:4)
320. A raven (Genesis 8:7)

Answer – Quiz 65

321. Israel (Lamentations 4:6)
322. Cedars (Song of Solomon 5:15)
323. Levites (1 Chronicles 15:2)
324. At the entrance gate (Joshua 20:4)
325. Jezebel (1 King 16:31)

Answer – Quiz 66

326. Noah, Daniel, and Job (Ezekiel 14:14)
327. Methuselah (Genesis 5:27)
328. To be ceremonially clean (Leviticus 13 & 14)
329. Land of Nod (Genesis 4:16)
330. Boaz married Ruth, and fathered Obed, who fathered Jesse, who fathered David (Ruth 4:13, 21-22)

Answer – Quiz 67

331. Ahasuerus was a king who reigned, from India even unto Ethiopia, over an hundred and twenty seven provinces (Esther 1:1)
332. Trumpets, pitchers/jars and torches/lamps (Judges 7:19-23)
333. Joshua (Joshua 10:12)
334. Psalm 23:1
335. Son of the governor (Haggai 1:14; 2:2)

Answer – Quiz 68

336. Seven priests (Joshua 6:8-13)
337. Zipporah (Exodus 2:21)
338. He arose from the ground, washed and anointed himself, and changed his clothes; and he went into the house of the Lord and worshiped. Then he went to his own house; and when he requested, they set food before him, and he ate. (2 Samuel 12:20)
339. Ezekiel, Hosea
340. Adonijah (1 Kings 1:5)

Answer – Quiz 69

341. A continual dripping on a very rainy day (Proverbs 27:15)
342. Hannah (1 Samuel 1:20)
343. Balaam (Numbers 22:28)
344. The House of Jacob (Obadiah 1:17)
345. Three (Genesis 6:10)

Answer – Quiz 70

346. From the beginning of creation (Genesis 1:1) to God's message to Malachi (1:1).
347. He was the son of Abraham's brother, Haran (Genesis 11:27)
348. Boaz (Ruth4:13)
349. The feast of tabernacles (Leviticus 23:34; Nehemiah 8:14)
350. The queen (Daniel 5:10-11)

Answer – Quiz 71

351. Enoch's rapture (Genesis 5:24, before the great flood) (Elia's ascension occurred only in 2 Kings 2:11)
352. 140 years (Job 42:16)
353. Midian (Exodus 2:15)
354. Esther (Esther 9:13)
355. Nabal (1 Samuel 25:3)

Answer – Quiz 72

356. A mountain (Exodus 3:1)
357. Nahor, and Haran. (Genesis 11:26)
358. He became Elijah's servant (1 Kings 19:19-21)
359. Reuben (Genesis 37:21-22)
360. King in Jerusalem (2 Kings 21:1)

Answer – Quiz 73

361. She was a harlot (Joshua 2:1)
362. Barnabas (Acts 9:27)
363. Anger (Genesis 4:5)
364. 365 years (Genesis 5:23)
365. One

Answer – Quiz 74

366. Noah (Genesis 8:8)
367. Jeroboam, (22 years – 2 Kings 14:20)
368. Isaiah (2 Kings 9:2); Jeremiah (2 Chronicles 36:12) Ezekiel (Ezekiel 1:3)
369. Acts
370. Judgement

Answer – Quiz 75

371. They did nothing
372. Pottery (1 Chronicles 4:23)
373. His father was Noah and his brothers were Shem and Japheth (Genesis 6:10)
374. Hezekiah (2 Kings 20:10)
375. Michal (1 Samuel 18:26)

Answer – Quiz 76

376. Moses' parents (Exodus 6:20)
377. Sweet, gravel (Proverbs 20:17)
378. Solomon (1 Kings 4:30)
379. Enoch (Genesis 5:6)
380. A certain woman cast a millstone on Abimelech's head and crushed his skull. (Judges 9:53)

Answer – Quiz 77

381. The Ark of the Covenant (2 Chronicles 1:4)
382. Peniel (Genesis 32:30)
383. He was brought there as a captive (Daniel 1:1-6)
384. King David (Psalm 23;1)
385. Thirty one (Joshua 12:24)

Answer – Quiz 78

386. More stupid than any man (Poverbs 30:2)
387. "Jehovah is there".
388. King Solomon (1 Kings 3:14)
389. Reuben (Genesis 29:32)
390. Jericho (Joshua 6:1-27)

Answer – Quiz 79

391. Rachel (Genesis 29:30)
392. That their son, Solomon, would be king (1 Kings 1:17)
393. "God Almighty" (Genesis 17:1) (El = God; Shaddai = Almighty. See ASV, ISV, KJV, NKJV, YLT)
394. Michal, David's wife (2 Samuel 3:14)
395. Orpah (Ruth 1:3-4)

Answer – Quiz 80

396. After having been weaned (1 Samuel 1:24; 2: 2:11)
397. He loved David greatly and made him his armor bearer. (1 Samuel 16:21)
398. The queen of Sheba, to king Solomon (1 Kings 10:7)
399. The dream would be bad news for the king (Daniel 4:19)
400. They slew the sons of Zedekiah before his eyes, and put out the eyes of Zedekiah, and bound him with fetters of brass, and carried him to Babylon. (2 Kings 25:7)

Answer – Quiz 81

401. His household idols (Genesis 31:17)
402. Leah (Genesis 29:25)
403. Hosea (Hosea 1:2)
404. The chief-cupbearer (Genesis 40;9-13)

Answer – Quiz 82

405. The Lord (Lamentations 3:10)
406. They have murmured against God (Numbers 14:29-33)
407. A rib (Genesis 2:21)
408. Jeremiah (Jeremiah 2:1-2; 2 Chronicles 35:25)
409. Adino the Eznite; Eleazar the son of Dodo; Shammah the son of Agee (2 Samuel 23:8-11)
410. The Lord God (Ezekiel 46:1-3)

Answer – Quiz 83

411. Zeruiah (2 Samuel 17:25)
412. At the eldest brother's house (Job 1:13-15)
413. Baal and Ashtoreth (Judges 2:13)
414. He was very angry because the people were worshipping a golden idol (Exodus 32:19)
415. Rahab (Joshua 6:25)

Answer – Quiz 84

416. He was lame (2 Samuel 4:4)
417. He went and possessed it after queen Jezebel had Naboth killed. (1 Kings 21:1-16)
418. Rehoboam rashly threatened his people that he would multiply their troubles (1 Kings 12:1-19)
419. They have heard that no enemy could stand against Israel (Joshua 2:9-11)
420. Adam and Eve (the Covenant of works, Gen. 2:15–17)

Answer – Quiz 85

421. Happy is he (Proverbs 16:20)
422. In the book of Esther
423. Amazia (Amos 7:10)
424. of Jacob (Micah 4:2)
425. 1 Samuel

Answer – Quiz 86

426. "No more mercy". (Hosea 1:6)
427. Nun (Exodus 33:11)
428. "curse" (Malachi 4:6)
429. To write a song and teach it to the people of Israel (Deuteronomy 31:19)
430. When a man is newly married, he shall not go out with the army or be liable for any other public duty. He shall be free at home one year to be happy with his wife whom he has taken. (Deuteronomy 24:5)

Answer – Quiz 87

431. The sword to kill, the dogs to tear, and the birds of the air and the beasts of the earth to devour and destroy. (Jeremiah 15:3)
432. It must be given to the Levites as their inheritance (Numbers 18:20-24)
433. She hammered a peg into his temple (Judges 4:21)
434. "See, I have this day set you over the nations and over the kingdoms, to root out, and to pull down,... to build, and to plant." To Jeremiah (Jeremiah 1:10)
435. eagles, lions (2 Samuel 1:23)

Answer – Quiz 88

436. Job would send for his children and consecrate them, and he would rise early in the morning and offer burnt offerings according to the number of them all (Job 1:5)
437. Jachin & Boas (1 Kings 7:21)
438. Rebekah (Genesis 25:20)
439. The Levites (Numbers 7:5)

Answer – Quiz 89

440. They had not spoken of God what is right, as Job had (Job 42:7)
441. Adonijah asked that Abishag the Shunammite be given to him as wife. (1 Kings 2:17, 23-25)
442. He was very overweight (Judges 3:17)
443. A priest and a scribe (Ezra 7:11)
444. "Holy to Yahweh" (Exodus 39:30; Leviticus 8:9)
445. His brother Aaron (Exodus 4:10-16)

Answer – Bonus Quiz

446. Proverbs 25:11
447. Through sacrifices (Leviticus 4:26)
448. King David gave instructions that he be put in the most dangerous part of the battle and then be left alone /withdrawn from (2 Samuel 11:15)

New Testament

TRIVIA

Quiz 1

1. What was Jesus' mother tongue?
2. When the apostles were giving food out to the widows, how many deacons did they select to assist them?
3. Whose delegates wanted to interrogate John when he was conducting baptisms out in the wild?
4. In what way did Jesus go to Heaven, from Earth?
5. Paul advised all congregants to bring certain things to church when they gather to worship. Which of the following did he not include? A hymn, a gift of leadership, a word of instruction, a revelation, a tongue or an interpretation?

Quiz 2

6. While Jesus was spreading his message, he advised that children should not come closer. True or false?
7. Cornelius, a centurion in the Italian army, was brought a message by whom?
8. How many books does the New Testament consist of?
9. What is the name of the "author and finisher of our faith", as mentioned in Hebrews?
10. What astonishing wonder, relating to languages, occurred during Peter's sermon at Pentecost?

Quiz 3

11. The Lord's Prayer consists of how many requests?
12. Before he started to follow Jesus, what vocation did St Luke pursue?
13. Which prophet was swallowed by a large fish?
14. According to Paul, what "abounds more and more in knowledge and in all judgement"?
15. How many brothers of Jesus does the Bible mention by name?

Quiz 4

16. While hanging on the cross, how many sayings did Jesus utter?
17. Which of Jesus' acquaintances wore a coat of camel hair, and had a meal of locusts and wild honey?
18. Jesus predicted that Peter would glorify God by becoming a martyr for him. True or False?
19. Is this true or false: "During the day following the birth of Jesus, the wise men arrived in Bethlehem"?
20. The tax collector Zacchaeus climbed into what type of tree to be able to see Jesus?

Quiz 5

21. Out of how many lepers that were healed by Jesus, did only a single one come back?
22. Who was the main author of the books comprising the New Testament?
23. Jesus was unaware that he would be seized and murdered in Jerusalem. True or False?
24. What are the words of the shortest Bible verse?
25. What were God the Father's words after the baptism of Jesus?

Quiz 6

26. What made Jesus weep in the shortest verse in the Bible?
27. For what reason was Jesus sentenced to death by Pontius Pilate, on Good Friday?
28. Who has the "power of death"?
29. Whom does 1 Corinthians call "the last Adam"?
30. To what nation did Paul belong?

Quiz 7

31. Ten men were cured of what sickness by Jesus?
32. There are nine Fruits of the Spirit, can you name at least one?
33. What was the wealthy young leader unwilling to part with?
34. What items did Jesus divide, to feed the crowd of about five thousand men, besides women and children?
35. Which books of the Bible have only a single chapter each?

Quiz 8

36. Jesus' Sermon on the Mount appears in which New Testament book?
37. By amount of devotees, which religion is the biggest on earth?
38. Collectively, what are Jesus' tales called?
39. After Jesus cured the man with the withered hand, who did the Pharisees team up with to kill him?
40. What book does the New Testament start with?

Quiz 9

41. Which two languages were the Old and New Testaments mostly written in?
42. Whose words were, "He is not here, for He is risen"?
43. What was the name of the river that Jesus was baptized in?
44. John the Baptist ate what type of creature in the desert?
45. Which book is thought to be the first of Paul's written letters?

Quiz 10

46. According to the Lord's Prayer, what food do we ask God for?
47. When Jesus was born, who ruled Judea?
48. When Jesus returned from Egypt, where did he spend his childhood?
49. In the tale of the Good Samaritan, the injured man was passed by a tax collector, an innkeeper, a priest and a judge. Which of these came first?
50. What was the name of Jesus' earthly father?

Quiz 11

51. Is the following true or false? "When Jeremiah was a grown man, God decided to call him as a prophet"
52. It was believed that one of the disciples would never die - who was it?
53. Is it true or false that Jesus declared the Old Testament rules to be irrelevant?
54. What is the fifth request in the Lord's Prayer,?
55. Whilst en route to Gaza, which Apostle told the Gospel to an Ethiopian officer?

Quiz 12

56. In which place did Jesus walk on water?
57. Who was the prodigal person according to Jesus' parable?
58. Name the three things that occurred at the moment of Jesus' death.
59. In which city was Jesus of Nazareth born?
60. What is the second request in the Lord's Prayer?

Quiz 13

61. Peter had a vision of animals clean and unclean - what did it mean?
62. When Zacchaeus the tax collector was saved, what portion of his riches did he donate to charity?
63. "What is the first request in the Lord's Prayer?
64. While moving through Galilee, what else did Jesus do apart from preaching?
65. What word does the New Testament end with?

Quiz 14

66. What did Herod say to the wise men, he wanted to do with Jesus?
67. How was Jesus killed?
68. Which leader suffered from leprosy?
69. What was the name of the tax collector who scaled a tree in order to see Jesus?
70. When Jesus died, what happened to the curtain inside the temple?

Quiz 15

71. 1 Thessalonians, complete the verse: "Pray without _____."
72. What are the names of the first two apostles to follow Jesus?
73. How many days did Mary and Joseph spend searching for Jesus when they went back to Jerusalem?
74. Complete the missing words, according to Hebrews: God's word is _____ and _____ .
75. Which disciple was described as being "of little faith"?

Quiz 16

76. Complete the missing words, according to Revelation: Jesus says: "Do not be afraid. I am the _____ and the _____."
77. Which of the Bible books is believed to be the last one that was written?
78. Which apostle renounced Jesus three times after his capture?
79. Where in the Bible is the Fruit of the Spirit listed?
80. During Jesus' baptism, whose voice was heard from the sky?

Quiz 17

81. Who did Paul say would be judged by the saints of Christ?
82. Who wrote the most books in the Bible?
83. Which books in the Bible contains the Lord's Prayer?
84. Saul was permitted to bring a burnt offering to God. True or False?
85. When Paul lost his eyesight, where was he going?

Quiz 18

86. Which ruler was responsible for judging Jesus?
87. According to the Bible, who are to be "dignified, not double-tongued, not addicted to much wine"?
88. After Jesus' resurrection, who was the first person to talk to him?
89. After he rose from the dead, for how many days did Jesus appear to his disciples?
90. Which is the third book in the New Testament?

Quiz 19

91. In the Lord's Prayer, what is the sixth thing that is requested?
92. After being untruthful to the Apostles about their contribution, Ananias and Sapphira died. True or False?
93. John the Baptist's clothes were woven from goat hair. True or false?
94. Which New Testament book refers to the perseverance of Job?
95. Which king ordered Jesus to be murdered when he was just an infant?

Quiz 20

96. Which disciple did not want Jesus to wash his feet?
97. Which three of Jesus' disciples names start with the letter "J"?
98. Is it true or false that an Angel saved Peter when he was in jail?
99. In Jesus' parable, how many of each of the wise and foolish girls were there?
100. Jesus changed the water into wine. True or false?

Quiz 21

101. There are a few books that speak of the birth of Jesus, name one?
102. When the Spirit led Jesus into the wild, what happened to him?
103. Can you recite the verse John 14:6?
104. Where does Jesus say a lamp is to be placed for all to see?
105. Who was a tax collector before he became an apostle?

Quiz 22

106. Is Jesus the Christ a descendant of David?
107. Where was the man going who was cared for by the Good Samaritan? To Jericho (Luke 10:30)
108. How would Jesus have that true worshippers will worship God correctly? In spirit and in truth (John 4:23-24)
109. Who was referred to by Jesus, as the "Comforter".
110. What group does James mostly work with?

Quiz 23

111. What sign did Judas use to point Jesus out to be seized?
112. What work did Jesus do before he became a preacher?
113. What is the number of people in the crowd that was fed with two fishes and five loaves of bread?
114. What did Jesus do for the mother of Simon's wife, to cure her?
115. During which event in the New Testament, do all three entities of the Holy Trinity appear?

Quiz 24

116. During the baptism of Jesus, as what did the Spirit appear?
117. What event from the Bible is celebrated on Palm Sunday?
118. When the Holy Spirit fell on the disciples, what form did it take?
119. The Works of the Flesh, are the opposite of The Fruits of the Spirit. True or False?
120. Jesus accepted all people that obey God, as his real family. True or False?

Quiz 25

121. When Herod issued the order for the infant Jesus to be killed, where did his family take him?
122. Which group visited Jesus with presents after his birth?
123. Who assisted with supporting and caring for Jesus and his disciples during his earthly ministry?
124. In which New Testament book is Paul's conversion detailed?
125. At the court hearing before Jesus' crucifixion, how did Pilate demonstrate his own guilt?

Quiz 26

126. Of Jesus' siblings, how many of his sisters' names can be found in the Bible?
127. In which Bible book is Lydia of Thyatira's tale told?
128. Is it true or false, that Jesus avoided people of poor character?
129. In which book would you find the Sermon on the Mount, preached by Jesus?
130. Out of all Jesus' miracles, which was performed first?

Quiz 27

131. What does the Bible call the "root of all evil"?
132. How was Lazarus helped by Jesus?
133. In the Lord's Prayer, what request comes seventh?
134. What is the name of the Angel that spoke to Mary?
135. Who made a crown out of thorns, for Jesus to wear?

Quiz 28

136. What was the name of the very first Christian who was persecuted for his beliefs?
137. Which animal did Lady Godiva ride on, in a carving found in Coventry Cathedral?
138. Jesus occasionally used saliva while he was healing people. True or false?
139. The word "snow" appears how many times in the Bible?
140. How did Jesus summarize the Law and all the prophets?

Quiz 29

141. What did Matthew do for a living before being called to be Jesus' disciple?
142. In Ephesians 5, whom does Paul say Christians should imitate?
143. Jesus' earthly family attempted to end his ministry at first, calling him mad. True or false?
144. Who performed Jesus' baptism?
145. Dorcas was raised from the dead by Peter. True or false?

Quiz 30

146. While traveling to Rome, which island was Paul shipwrecked on?
147. Who was the third person who came upon the wounded man, in the story about the good Samaritan?
148. How many people observed Jesus after his resurrection?
149. In the story about the good Samaritan, who was the first person who came upon the wounded man?
150. In how many instances did Peter say that he did not know Jesus?

Quiz 31

151. During Jesus' arrest, which apostle amputated the ear of a soldier?
152. For how long was Jesus tempted in the desert?
153. By what other name was the apostle Paul known?
154. How many books does the Bible consist of?
155. How many books named after John exists?

Quiz 32

156. Which four books make up the Gospels?
157. Whose wives accompanied them during their evangelical missions?
158. Which four books outline the life of Jesus when he was on earth?
159. In which city was Jesus born?
160. Who is the brightness of God's glory, and the express image of his person,?

Quiz 33

161. Which of his disciples eventually betrayed Jesus?
162. What activity were Peter and Andrew busy with when they were asked by Jesus to accompany him?
163. What was Joseph, Jesus' earthly father, by trade?
164. Jesus was well-loved wherever he went, and all people trusted his word. True or false?
165. According to the New Testament, which person was shipwrecked?

Quiz 34

166. Jesus proclaimed that God only wanted large financial contributions. True or false?
167. What was the archangel called?
168. What object was placed to cover the entrance to Jesus' tomb, and had to be rolled away?
169. How long did Jesus' fast last, in days and nights?
170. What is the meaning of Jehovah Rapha?

Quiz 35

171. Whom does the sentence, "And he is the propitiation for our sins..." refer to?
172. Which two items does the woman use to wash Jesus' feet, in the book of Luke?
173. Which man referred to himself as a "Hebrew of the Hebrews"?
174. Jesus was not maltreated before He was crucified. True or False.
175. Which man's sight was restored by Jesus?

Quiz 36

176. In which way did Paul manage to get out of Damascus?
177. What was God's message when he spoke from the sky during Jesus' baptism?
178. Who bought Joseph when his brothers sold him as a slave?
179. Which man said, "How long will you waver between two opinions?"
180. What is the name of the site of Jesus' crucifixion?

Quiz 37

181. Who chooses the pope during an election?
182. By what name is Christ's holy cup known?
183. At Simon the Leper's home, what liquid did the woman spill over Jesus' feet?
184. Who did Paul say should be educated to not talk back?
185. Which book of the Bible was written by Jesus himself?

Quiz 38

186. Which cousin of Jesus was the most well-known?
187. Complete the missing word: "In addition to all this, take up your shield of _____, with which you can extinguish all the flaming arrows of the evil one."
188. Jesus condemned eating with unwashed hands. True or false?
189. Who instructed people in the Lord's prayer?
190. During the Last Supper, what act did Jesus do for the disciples?

Quiz 39

191. With which book does the New Testament end?
192. Which man undertook teaching missions to spread the word to the Gentiles?
193. Which commandment does Jesus proclaim as the first and most important?
194. An apple is a fruit of the Spirit. True or false?
195. How long did Lazarus lay dead for, prior to Jesus resurrecting him?

Quiz 40

196. Who was the man who ministered at Pentecost?
197. In the course of his teachings in the city of Joppa, where did Peter stay?
198. Who authored Galatians?
199. When he was in the Gerasenes, what evil being was cast out by Jesus?
200. Who did Christ give his life for, according to Romans?

Quiz 41

201. The Jewish rulers wanted to set Jesus free. True or false?
202. In what way does Judas show the Roman soldiers who Jesus is?
203. What was the total number of apostles that were with Jesus?
204. Jesus had no siblings. True or false?
205. From which family's lineage did Paul come?

Quiz 42

206. By which Jerusalem high priest was Jesus placed on trial?
207. Paul dreamed that someone had told him to go to Carthage. True or false?
208. How does the verse 1 Corinthians 13:4 go?
209. What relative of Jesus warned, "Repent, for the Kingdom of Heaven is at hand"?
210. Following Jesus' burial in the tomb, what event took place?

Quiz 43

211. To what does Paul liken the church?
212. On which day of the week did the resurrection of Jesus take place?
213. Can you name one of Jesus' four brothers?
214. How long after the resurrection, did Jesus go to Heaven?
215. Which religious elders were constantly attempting to ambush Jesus with their interrogations?

Quiz 44

216. How many baskets of fish and bread remained after Jesus fed the 5000+ strong crowd?
217. Complete the verse from James 4: "What causes fights and quarrels among you?
218. Which Bible book is the shortest?
219. The armor of God consists of several parts. Which of these is not correct? Is it the belt of truth, shield of knowledge, sword of the Spirit or helmet of salvation?
220. What did the prison officer from Philippi ask Paul before the Gospel was preached to him?

Quiz 45

221. Which apostle was known as the Apostle to the Jewish people?
222. Where was the term "Christians" first used, referring to Jesus' devotees?
223. In the Lord's Prayer, what is requested fourth?
224. Jesus was able to resurrect people from the dead during his time on Earth. True or false?
225. Which person was banished to stay on an island?

226. What profession did Simon have prior to becoming an apostle?
227. What do we ask for third, according to the Lord's Prayer?
228. What does Jesus command regarding judging people around us?
229. Whose words were, "Peace, be still"?
230. When do we celebrate Christmas?

Quiz 47

231. On which Sea did Jesus quiet down a storm?
232. After the Last Supper, in which garden did Jesus go to pray?
233. Which animals frequently feature as a means of transportation in the Bible?
234. When Jesus resurrected Lazarus, which two things did he do?
235. Which of the twelve disciples had a sick mother-in-law, who was cured by Jesus?

Quiz 48

236. The Book Hebrews that Jesus deserves more glory than this Old Testament person. Who is this person?
237. In which Bible book is the story of the three Wise Men's encounter with the infant Jesus described?
238. Jesus was asked questions by which person who belonged to the Jewish governing committee?
239. What happened to Jesus 40 days after he was raised from the dead?
240. Which Apostle traveled to Samaria to teach God's word?

Quiz 49

241. Who was Jesus' earthly mother?
242. When Paul and Silas were jailed in Philippi, God stirred an earthquake to set them free. True or false?
243. Which priestly department was Zechariah registered under, according to the Gospel of Luke?
244. How many church congregations did John address in his writing?
245. Who foretold Jesus' coming just before it happened?

Quiz 50

246. After the crucifixion, who requested Jesus' body from Pilate?
247. Which other person from the New Testament has his teachings cited in the book of 2 Peter?
248. Who was the grandmother of Timotheus?
249. Who were Jacob's mother and grandmother?
250. What event from the Old Testament are we reminded of in Jude?

Quiz 51

251. Which two men were "given to Satan" due to their blasphemy?
252. Wo are children of God according to the book of Galatians?
253. What distinctive method of storytelling does Jesus use in the Gospels, to spread his word?
254. In which way did Jesus identify the person who would give him away?
255. Of which person was Paul speaking when he said "mine own bowels"?

Quiz 52

256. When the infant Jesus was introduced at the Temple, who identified him as the Messiah?
257. On Herod's birthday, who did he hold a celebration for?
258. "Charity suffereth long, and is kind; charity envieth not; charity vaunteth not itself, is not puffed up." Where in the Bible is this verse located?
259. Whom did Paul write to Philemon about?
260. How does Paul refer to Philemon?

Quiz 53

261. How many times is the Lord's Prayer outlined in the Bible?
262. Before he started preaching, what was Paul of Tarsus called?
263. Who did Paul urge the Corinthians not to participate with?
264. Can you recite the verse 2 Corinthians 5:20?
265. Which people does Jesus want us to ask to our banquet, in Luke 14?

Quiz 54

266. With which method was Stephanus killed?
267. In which place did a prison-keeper become faithful?
268. Which man does John describe as "the disciple Jesus loved"?
269. What organ is referred to in this verse: "Consider what a great forest is set on fire by a small spark."
270. Who was Bernice?

Quiz 55

271. Which event occurred first, the feeding of 5000 people, or John's beheading?
272. What is the correct stand to take regarding the Word of Truth, according to James?
273. Whose words are these: "Lord, shew us the Father, and it sufficeth us"?
274. What was the place called where the crucifixion took place?
275. How does this saying by Jesus end?

Quiz 56

276. How many chapters are in Jeremiah, and how many verses are in the letter of Jude?
277. When Jesus went to his hometown, what was he shocked by?
278. Once Paul found out about the Ephesians' love and belief, what did he not cease doing?
279. After the birth of Jesus, who were the first people to be told?
280. At what place did Jesus and the Samaritan woman have a conversation?

Quiz 57

281. Like what kind of person, was Timothy motivated to experience difficulties, by Paul?
282. According to the Beatitudes, what kind of people will be filled?
283. In which place did Jesus first openly deliver a sermon, according to the Gospel of Matthew?
284. Who was John the Baptist's father?
285. When Peter was imprisoned by Herod so that he could be given to the Jews to be killed, who saved him?

Quiz 58

286. Which people was the book of Romans written for?
287. What were Jesus' brothers names?
288. Paul went to Jerusalem to see whom?
289. When Jesus took on his heavenly body, which two people from the Old Testament were with him?
290. Who did Peter write his initial letter to?

Quiz 59

291. How long did Paul stay in Damascus after he became a believer?
292. What did the council of Apostles in Jerusalem decide, should be abstained from the Old Testament?
293. Which prophet from the Old Testament is repeatedly mentioned in Romans?
294. According to Hebrews 11, how many instances of exhibits of belief from the Old Testament are named?
295. The Romans displayed what quality, which was talked about all over the world?

Quiz 60

296. What was the name of Priscilla's husband, and what work did he do?
297. Who's wife did Herod marry?
298. Which Roman serviceman was meant to have stabbed Jesus?
299. To motivate people to be patient for when the Lord Jesus returns, what does James use as a model?
300. Crete can be struck by extreme storm winds, what are they called?

Quiz 61

301. Which disciple was the treasurer for Jesus and the disciples?
302. Which person was Paul's co-author with the letter to the Philippians?
303. What did Herod say to Herodias' daughter, she could have for her pleasing dance?
304. When the disciples were holding sermons on Pentecost, what did the crowd say to jeer them?
305. For whom should the Corinthians' freedom not be a stumbling block?

Quiz 62

306. From which place did Jesus go to heaven?
307. When they observed the man who was taken over by the legion of demons being cured, how did the people act?
308. Who does not use the door to go into the sheep pen, according to Jesus?
309. Which person was chosen by the Holy Spirit to go with Paul, while he was praying at the church in Antioch?
310. Which people did James and John desire to destroy with fire?

Quiz 63

311. Which event occurred first, the feeding of the 5000 people, or the baptism of Jesus?
312. Which two disciples started following Jesus first?
313. What was Epaphroditus known for?
314. Which of the Gospels was authored by a physician?
315. In the New Testament, which book is the shortest?

Quiz 64

316. What trait did the possessed man have who lived among the graves?
317. Whom was 3 John written for?
318. Who saved Paul from those who were harassing him?
319. What happened to the disciples when Jesus woke and told the storm to cease?
320. When the storm broke out on the Sea of Galilee while Jesus and the disciples were going across, where was Jesus?

Quiz 65

321. In the book of Titus, whose "mouths must be stopped"?
322. In 1 and 2 Thessalonians, who spoke to the people, apart from Paul?
323. How were the disciples sent out to preach without Jesus?
324. Where did the man who was possessed by a legion of demons, relate his tale?
325. Which three evangelists are named in the Bible?

Quiz 66

326. Why was Jesus taken to Egypt as an infant, by his parents?
327. When the Corinthians started arguing, who told Paul?
328. Apart from Paul and Timothy, which other missionary told the story of Christ to the Corinthians?
329. Who was the Philippian girl haunted by?
330. For how many years did Paul teach at the school of Tyrannus at Ephesus, during his third evangelical trip?

Quiz 67

331. What did the people whom James was addressing, strongly believe in?
332. In which place is "Satan's throne" found?
333. What is the number of pilgrims that made the journey to Santiago in 2016?
334. Who was Jesus speaking of here: "Among those born of women there is not a greater prophet n"
335. How did the woman who had been suffering from bloodletting for twelve years, get cured?

Quiz 68

336. When Jairus requested of Jesus to heal his daughter, how did Jesus respond?
337. Which word is written more than 46,000 times in the Bible?
338. After how many years did Paul relocate back to Jerusalem?
339. Who stood against Moses, and was later used to compare dishonest and averse men to, by Paul?
340. Which man accompanied Paul when he first went out to preach?

Quiz 69

341. What did the tenants do to the son of the vineyard owner, according to the story?
342. Can you recite Romans 1, verse 20 and 21?
343. Who was jailed with Paul, in the book of Philemon?
344. After Jesus freed the man of the legion of demons and sent them into the pigs, what did the Gadarenes ask him to do?
345. Which book in the Bible comes after John?

346. Which person authored the Acts of the Apostles?
347. What did the Corinthians think of Paul, based on the letters he wrote?
348. How does this saying by Jesus end?
349. In which book are the evangelical missions of Paul told?
350. When interrogated over his rights in the temple courts, what did Jesus ask the head priests, instructors and elders?

Quiz 71

351. "Jesus I know, and Paul I know; but who are ye?" Who was speaking here?
352. How did Jesus' interrogators react when He responded to their questions related to taxes?
353. Who wrote down the dictation of the author of the book of Romans?
354. When Peter was addressing the people at Pentecost, which two people from the Old Testament did he speak of?
355. Where was John when the vision of Revelation was given to him?

Quiz 72

356. What did Peter see baptism as?
357. "His blood comes over us and our children"?
358. In which book of the Bible is this sentence: "Everything is possible for one who believes."?
359. At the time of Jesus' birth, who was the governor in Syria?
360. What kind of people crept in among the believers unnoticed, according to Jude?

Quiz 73

361. What action did the governor of Damascus want to take against Paul?
362. Which person was given thirty pieces of silver, as payment for betrayal?
363. In which place did Paul leave his coat behind?
364. Give the names of three people who were jailed in the Bible.
365. Whom will Paul send to Titus?

Quiz 74

366. What was Jude's brother called?
367. When Paul tried to go back to visit the Thessalonians, who tried to stop him?
368. Who wrote the Book of Revelation?
369. Which man eventually killed John the Baptist?
370. Who was the author of 1 and 2 Peter?

Quiz 75

371. What were the names of Zebadee's two sons?
372. The secret and persona of Jesus is dealt with most in which Gospel?
373. Which goddess in Ephesus was adored the most?
374. In which place was Jesus apprehended?
375. Which disciple discovered a coin inside a fish's mouth?

Quiz 76

376. Where were Paul and Silas jailed during their second evangelical mission?
377. Who was speaking here, and to whom: "It won't take much more for you to convince to become a Christian"?
378. Which legal practitioner is spoken of in the book of Titus?
379. Of what natural material are the twelve gates of New Jerusalem constructed, according to Revelation?
380. What is Stephen's relevance in Acts of the Apostles?

Quiz 77

381. Who was dispatched to the Ephesians by Paul?
382. Which event occurred first, the appointment of Matthew as an apostle, or the appearance of the Holy Spirit?
383. In which Gospel are the least amount of Jesus' miracles chronicled?
384. What does 1 Timothy 2 verse 4 say?
385. Which nation's tolerance and belief in times of oppression does Paul brag about to the other churches?

Quiz 78

386. Which apostle did not believe that Jesus was raised from the dead, until he saw him for himself?
387. Fill in the missing word: "In every battle you will need faith as your _____ to stop the fiery arrows aimed at you by Satan."
388. What made the woman from Syrophonecia approach Jesus?
389. Which of the everlasting qualities is the greatest, as set out in 1 Corinthians?
390. What became of the souls of people who were beheaded because they were believers, according to John's notes in Revelation?

New Testament

TRIVIA

Answers

Answers – Quiz 1

1. Aramaic (Mark 15:34)
2. Seven (Acts 6:1-6)
3. Pharisees' (John 1:24).
4. He rose and a cloud took him out of their sight (Acts 1:9)
5. A gift of leadership (1 Corinthians 1:26).

Answers – Quiz 2

6. False (Matthew 19:14; Mark 10:30; Luke 18:16)
7. An angel. (Acts 10:1-8)
8. 27 books
9. Jesus (Hebrews 12:2)
10. The people heard the disciples talking in languages which they (the disciples themselves) did not know (Acts 2:6-12)

Answers – Quiz 3

11. Seven (Matthew 6:9-13; Luke 11:2-4).
12. Medical doctor (Colossians 4:14).
13. Jonah (Jonah 1:17)
14. Love (Philippians 1:9).
15. Four. (Mark 6:3)

16.   Seven cross words.
1. Father, forgive them; for they know not what they do (Luke 23:34).
2. Today you will be with me in paradise (Luke 23:43)
3. Woman, behold, thy son! Behold, thy mother! (John 19:26) When Jesus saw his mother and the disciple whom he loved standing nearby, he said to his mother, "Woman, behold, your son!" :27 Then he said to the disciple, "Behold, your mother!" And from that hour the disciple took her to his own home.
4. My God, my God, why hast thou forsaken me? (Matthew 27:46 & Mark 15:34)
5. I thirst (John 19:28)
6. It is finished (John 19:30)
7. Father, into thy hands I commend my spirit (Luke 23:4)

17.   John the Baptist (Matthews 3:4)

18.   True (John 21:18-19)

19.   False. They arrived during the same night that Jesus was born and followed the star to where he had been born. (Matthew 2:9)

20.   He climbed into a sycamore tree (Luke 19:4).

21.   10 lepers (Luke10:12-18).

22.   The Holy Spirit inspired all the authors of the Bible, and is thus the main Author. St. Paul authored most of the books of the New Testament.

23.   False. He repeatedly foretold it to his disciples – (Matthew 16:21; 17:22-23; 20:18) – echoed in the gospel according to Mark, Luke and John.

24.   "Jesus wept" (John 11:35)

25.   "This is my beloved Son, in whom I am well pleased (/ in whom I delight). (Matthew 3:17).

Answers – Quiz 6

26. When Jesus saw Lazarus sister weeping, and the Jews who had come with her also weeping, he was deeply moved in his spirit and greatly troubled (John 11:33).
27. He was falsely accused of calling himself the king of the Jews (John 19:2-3)
28. The devil (Hebrews 2:14)
29. (1 Corinthians 15:45) Jesus Christ (Romans 5:12-21)
30. He was a Jew/Israelite (Philippians 3:5)

Answers – Quiz 7

31. Leprosy (Luke 17:12-14)
32. Love, joy, peace, patience, kindness, goodness, faithfulness, gentleness, self-control (Galatians 5:22-23)
33. His great possessions (Mark 10:22)
34. Five loaves of bread and two fishes (Matthew 14:16-21)
35. John, Titus, Habakkuk or Obadiah? Obadiah in the Old Testament and Jude in the New Testament.

Answers – Quiz 8

36. Matthew chapters 5-7.
37. Christianity (33%)
38. Parables (Matthew 13:13-14)
39. The Herodians (Mark 3:6)
40. The Gospel according to Matthew

Answers – Quiz 9

41. The Old Testament was written mainly in Hebrew (a small part in Aramaic), and the whole New Testament in Greek.
42. The angel at the empty tomb of Jesus (Matthew 28:2)
43. The river Jordan (Matthew 3:13)
44. Locusts and wild honey (Mark 1:6)
45. There is no certainty. The first epistle to the Thessalonians is thought to have been written in 48-55 AD, while the letter to the Galatians may have been written 49-55 AD.

Answers – Quiz 10

46. Bread (Matthew 6:11)
47. Herod (Matthew 2:1)
48. Nazareth (Matthew 2:23)
49. A priest (Luke 10:31)
50. Joseph (Matthew 1:16, 20)

Answers – Quiz 11

51. False. God decided to call Jeremiah as a prophet long before he was born. (Jeremiah 1:4-5)
52. John (John 21:20-24) (John, the author of this book, sometimes called himself "the disciple whom Jesus loved".)
53. False. He said that he had come to fulfill it. (Matthew 5:17)
54. "Forgive us our debts" (Luke 11:4)
55. Philip (Acts 8:26-35)

Answers – Quiz 12

56. The sea of Galilee (Matthews 14:22-27)
57. A father's son (Luke 15:11-24)
58. The curtain in the temple was torn in two, an earthquake occurred, and graves opened and the resurrected ones walked (Matthew 27:50-52)
59. Bethlehem (Luke 2:4-7; Matthew 2:1)
60. Thy kingdom come (Matthew 6:10)

Answers – Quiz 13

61. It meant that to the Gentiles also God has granted repentance that leads to life. (Acts 11:18)
62. Half of his goods (Luke 19:8)
63. "Hallowed be thy Name" (Luke 11:2)
64. He healed every disease and every affliction among the people and cast out demons. (Matthew 4:23; Mark 1:39)
65. "Amen". (Revelation 22:21)

Answers – Quiz 14

66. He said he would also go and worship him (Matthew 2:8)
67. Crucified (Matthew 27:35; Mark 15:24 etc.)
68. Naaman (2 Kings 5:1)
69. Zacchaeus. (Luke 19:4)
70. It was torn in two, from top to bottom (Mat 27:51)

Answers – Quiz 15

71. Pray without ceasing (1 Thes.5:17).
72. Simon Peter and his brother Andrew (Matthew 4:18-20)
73. Three days (Luke 2:41-46)
74. Alive and active (Hebrews 4:12)
75. The apostle Peter (Matthew 14:28- 31)

Answers – Quiz 16

76. First and the Last (Revelation 1:17)
77. 2 Peter
78. Peter (Luke 22:54-62)
79. Galatians 5:22-23
80. God the Father's voice (Matthew 3:17)

Answers – Quiz 17

81. The world (1 Corinthians 6:2)
82. Paul (wrote 13 books)
83. Matthew 6 and Luke 11
84. False. Only priests were permitted to make any sacrifice to God. (1 Samuel 13:9-13)
85. Damascus (Acts 9:3-8)

Answers – Quiz 18

86. Pilate (Mark 15:15:15)
87. Deacons (1 Timothy 3:8)
88. Mary Magdalene (Mark 16:9)
89. Forty days (Acts 1:3)
90. The Gospel according to Luke

Answers – Quiz 19

91. Lead us not into temptation, but deliver us from evil (Matthew 6:13)
92. True (Acts 5:5-10)
93. False (Mark 1:6)
94. James 5:11
95. Herod (Matthew 2:16)

Answers – Quiz 20

96. Peter (John 13:8)
97. John and James (Matthew 4:21) and Judas (Matthew 10:4)
98. False (Acts 16:25-26)
99. 5 wise and 5 foolish (Matthews 25:2)
100. True (John 2:1-11)

Answers – Quiz 21

101. The Gospel according to Luke (2:1-7)
102. He was tempted by the devil (Matthew 4:1)
103. In my Father's house are many mansions: if it were not so, I would have told you. I go to prepare a place for you.
104. On a lampstand (Matthew 5:15)
105. Matthew (Matthew 9:9; 10:3)

Answers – Quiz 22

106. Yes (Matthew 1:1)
107. To Jericho (Luke 10:30)
108. In spirit and in truth (John 4:23-24)
109. God the Holy Spirit (John 14:16-17)
110. The twelve tribes which are scattered abroad (James 1:1)

Answers – Quiz 23

111. A kiss (Mark 14:44)
112. Carpentry (Mark 6:3)
113. 5,000, women and children excluded (Matthew 14:21)
114. Jesus healed her by touching her hand (Matthew 8:14-15)
115. At Jesus' baptism (Matthew 3:16-17)

Answers – Quiz 24

116. A dove (Matthew 3:16)
117. Jesus' entry into Jerusalem on the day before his crucifixion (Matthew 21:1-11)
118. Tongues like flames of fire (Acts 2:3)
119. True (Galatians 5:19-23)
120. True (Mark 3:35)

Answers – Quiz 25

121. To Egypt (Matthew 2:13-14)
122. Wise men from the East (Matthew 2:1-11)
123. Some women who had been healed of evil spirits and illnesses: Mary, also called Magdalene, from whom seven demons had gone out; Joanna, the wife of Herod's household manager Chuza; Susanna; and many others. These women continued to support them out of their personal resources. (Luke 8:2-3)
124. Acts 9:1-6
125. He washed his hands, saying, I am innocent of the blood of this just person. (Matthew 27:24)

Answers – Quiz 26

126. None
127. Acts (16:14-15)
128. False (Mark 2:16)
129. Matthew chapters 5-7
130. Changed water into wine (John 2:11)

Answers – Quiz 27

131. The love of money (1 Timothy 6:10)
132. Jesus called him to life after he had died (John 11:43-44)
133. "Deliver us from evil". (Luke 11:4)
134. Gabriel (Luke 1:26-27)
135. The Roman soldiers (John 19:2)

Answers – Quiz 28

136. Stephen (Acts 7:59)
137. A goat
138. True (Mark 8:23)
139. 24 times.
140. "You shall love the Lord your God with all your heart and with all your soul and with all your mind. This is the great and first commandment. And a second is like it: You shall love your neighbor as yourself. On these two commandments depend all the Law and the Prophets." (Matthew 22:37-40)

Answers – Quiz 29

141. He was a tax collector (Matthew 10:3)
142. God (Ephesians 5:1)
143. False (Luke 2:47-52)
144. John the Baptist (Mark 1:9)
145. True (Acts 9:40)

Answers – Quiz 30

146. Malta (Acts 28:1)
147. A Samaritan (Luke 10:31-33)
148. More than 100 (1 Corinthians 15:1-6)
149. A Priest (Luke 10:31)
150. Three time (Matthew 26:69-74)

Answers – Quiz 31

151. Peter (John 18:10)
152. 40 days (Mark 1:13)
153. Saul of Tarsus (Acts 9:11)
154. 66
155. Four: The Gospel according to John, and Johns three letters, 1, 2 and 3 John

Answers – Quiz 32

156. Matthew, Mark, Luke & John.
157. The apostles and the brothers of the Lord and Cephas (1 Corinthians 9:5)
158. The Gospel according to Matthew, Mark, Luke & John
159. Bethlehem (Matthew 2:1)
160. Jesus Christ, the Son of God (Hebrews 1:2-3)

Answers – Quiz 33

161. Judas Iscariot (Matthew 27:3-4)
162. Casting their nets into the sea (Matthew 4:18)
163. A Carpenter (Matthew 13:54-55)
164. False. The Pharisees and Scribes continually sought to kill him. (Matthew 26:3-4; Mark 9:31; Luke 13:31; John 5:18; 7:1 etc.)
165. Paul (2 Corinthians 11:25)

Answers – Quiz 34

166. False (Mark 12:41-44)
167. Michael (Jude 1:9)
168. A large stone (Matthew 27:60)
169. Forty (Matthew 4:2)
170. The Lord who heals

Answers – Quiz 35

171. Jesus Christ (1 John 4:10)
172. Her tears and hair (Luke 7:38)
173. Paul (Philippians 3:5)
174. False (John 19:1-3).
175. Bartimaeus (Mark 10:46)

Answers – Quiz 36

176. He was lowered down the outer wall in a basket (Acts 9:23-25)
177. "This is my beloved Son, with whom I am well pleased." (Matthew 3:17)
178. Ishmaelites (Genesis 37:28)
179. Elijah (1 Kings 18:21)
180. Golgotha (Mark 15:21-24)

Answers – Quiz 37

181. Cardinals
182. The holy grail
183. Her tears (Luke 7:38, 44)
184. Servants (Titus 2:9)
185. Not one

Answers – Quiz 38

186. John the Baptist
187. Faith. (Ephesians 6:16)
188. False (Matthew 15:20)
189. Jesus (Matthew 6:9)
190. He washed their feet (John 13:5)

Answers – Quiz 39

191. Revelation
192. Paul (Book of Acts)
193. Love God with all your heart, soul and mind (Matthew 22:37-38)
194. False (Galatians 5:22-23)
195. 4 days (John 11:17)

Answers – Quiz 40

196. Peter (Acts 2:14)
197. With Simon, a tanner (Acts 9:43)
198. Paul (Galatians 1:1)
199. An unclean spirit (Mark 5:1-13)
200. By one man's obedience many will be made righteous. (Romans 5:19)

Answers – Quiz 41

201. False (John 19:6)
202. He would kiss Jesus to identify him (Mark 14:44)
203. Twelve (Mark 10:2)
204. False (Matthew 13:55)
205. Posterity of Israel, tribe of Benjamin. (Romans 11:1)

Answers – Quiz 42

206. Caiaphas (Matthew 26:57)
207. False
208. "Love is patient, love is _____." "Love is patient and kind; love does not envy or boast; it is not arrogant"
209. John the Baptist (Matthew 3:1-2)
210. Guards were posted to guard his body. (Matthew 27:62-66)

Answers – Quiz 43

211. To a human body as the body of Christ (1 Corinthians 12:12-27)
212. The 1st day (Matthew 28:1)
213. James and Joseph and Simon and Judas (Matthew 13:55)
214. 40 days (Acts 1:3)
215. Scribes and Pharasees. (Matthew 12:14, 38; 15:1-2; Mark 2:16, etc.)

Answers – Quiz 44

216. Twelve baskets (Matthew 14:20)
217. Don't they come from your _____ that battle within you? You want something but don't get it." Passions (James 4:1)
218. 3rd letter of John
219. Shield of knowledge (Ephesians 6:16)
220. "what must I do to be saved?" (Acts 16:30)

Answers – Quiz 45

221. Peter (1 Peter 1:1)
222. In Antioch (Acts 11:26)
223. "Give us this day our daily bread" (Luke 11:3)
224. True (John 11:42-43)
225. The disciple John (Revelation 1:9)

Answers – Quiz 46

226. Fisherman (Matthew 4:18)
227. "Your will be done" (Matthew 6:10)
228. Judge not (Luke 6:37)
229. Jesus' words (Mark 4:39)
230. 25th December

Answers – Quiz 47

231. The sea of Galilee (Luke 8:26)
232. Gethsemane (Matthew 26:36)
233. Donkeys and camels (**Donkeys**: Genesis 22:3; 44:13; Numbers 22:21; **Camels**: Genesis 24:64; 31:34; 37:25, etc.)
234. He wept, prayed, and called Lazarus out. (John 11:35-43)
235. Peter (Matthew 8:14)

Answers – Quiz 48

236. Moses. (Hebrews 10:28-29)
237. Matthew Chapter 2
238. Nicodemus (John 3:1-4)
239. He ascended to heaven. (Acts 1:39)
240. Phillip (Acts 8:5)

Answers – Quiz 49

241. Mary Magdalene (Matthews 1:16)
242. True (Acts 16:26)
243. Abijah (Luke 1:5)
244. Seven (Revelation 1:4).
245. John the Baptist (Matthew 3:11)

Answers – Quiz 50

246. Joseph of Arimathéa (Mark 15:43)
247. Paul (2 Peter 3:15-16)
248. Lois (2 Peter 3:16)
249. Rebecca and Sarah (Romans 9:10)
250. The exodus from Egypt (Jude 1:5)

Answers – Quiz 51

251. Hymenaeus and Alexander. (1 Timothy 1:20)
252. Those who have faith in Jesus Christ (Galations 3:26)
253. Parables.
254. It is one of the twelve, who dips with him in the dish. (Mark 14:20)
255. Onesimus (Philemon 1:12)

Answers – Quiz 52

256. Simeon (Luke 2:34)
257. Herod on his birthday gave a feast for his nobles, the high officers, and the chief men of Galilee. (Mark 6:21)
258. 1 Corinthians 13:4.
259. Onesimus (Philemon 1:10)
260. His child – meaning that Paul had led him to Chirst (Philemon 1:10)

Answers – Quiz 53

261. Twice. (Matthew 6:9; Luke 11:2)
262. Saul (Acts 9:4)
263. Demons (1 Corinthians 10:20-21)
264. Therefore, we are ambassadors for Christ, God making his appeal through us. We implore you on behalf of Christ, be reconciled to God.
265. The poor, the maimed, the lame & the blind (Luke 14:13)

Answers – Quiz 54

266. Stoning (Acts 7:59)
267. Philippi (Acts 16:12-33)
268. John (John 21:7, 20) It is known that John called himself so
269. The tongue (James 3:5-6)
270. The Bible does not say. Tradition would have it that she was either king Agrippa's daughter or his wife. (Acts 25:13, 23; 26:30)

Answers – Quiz 55

271. John's beheading (Matthew 14:10-21)
272. Be swift to hear, slow to speak, slow to wrath (James 1:19)
273. Philip (John 14:8)
274. Golgotha, meaning place of a skull. (Mark 15:22)
275. "Full well ye reject the commandment of God,..." that ye may keep your own tradition. (Mark 7:9)

Answers – Quiz 56

276. 52, and 25
277. Their lack of faith (Luke 4:16-28)
278. Giving thanks to god for them (Ephesians 1:16)
279. Shepherds (Luke 2:8-11)
280. Sychar (John 4:5-26)

Answers – Quiz 57

281. A soldier (2 Timothy 2:3)
282. Blessed are those who hunger and thirst for righteousness, For they shall be filled. (Matthew 5:6)
283. On a mount (Matthew chapters 5-7)
284. Zacharias (Luke 1:13)
285. An angel of the Lord (Acts 12:7-11)

Answers – Quiz 58

286. To all who are in Rome, beloved of God, called to be saints. (Romans 1:7)
287. James, and Joses, and Simon, and Judas. (Matthew 13:55)
288. Peter (Acts 1:18)
289. Moses and Elijah (Luke 9:29-30)
290. To the pilgrims of the Dispersion in Pontus, Galatia, Cappadocia, Asia, and Bithynia, elect according to the foreknowledge of God the Father, (1 Peter 1:1-2).

Answers – Quiz 59

291. Many days (Acts 9:23-25)
292. Abstain from things offered to idols, from blood, from things strangled, and from sexual immorality. (Acts 15:29)
293. Isaiah (Romans 9:27, 29; 10:16, 20; 15:12)
294. 23
295. Faith (Romans 1:8)

Answers – Quiz 60

296. Aquila, was a tent maker (Acts 18:2-3)
297. His brother Philip's wife, Herodias (Mark 6:17)
298. Longinius (not mentioned in the Bible)
299. A husbandman (James 5:7-8)
300. Euroklydon (no biblical source)

Answers – Quiz 61

301. Judas Iscariot Judas (John 12:6; 13:29)
302. Timothy (Philippians 1:1)
303. Anything she wanted, up to half of his kingdom (Mark 6:22-23)
304. That they are drunk (Acts 2:13)
305. For the weak (1 Corinthians 8:9)

Answers – Quiz 62

306. Mount Olivet (Acts 1:6-12)
307. They fled (Mark 5:14)
308. Thieves and robbers (John 10:1)
309. Barnabas (Acts 13:1-3)
310. Samaritan villagers (Luke 9:54)

Answers – Quiz 63

311. The baptism of Jesus was first (Matthew 3:13-15) 5000 men fed (Matthew 6:44)
312. Simon Peter and Andrew (Matthew 4:18)
313. Paul's fellow worker, fellow soldier, minister of Paul's needs, longing for the believers in Philippi, brought gifts from the Philippians to Paul (Philippians 2:25-27; 4:18)
314. Luke was a physician (Colossians 4:14) and he authored both the Gospel according to Luke and Acts, dedicating both to the governor Theophilus (Acts 1:1)
315. 2 John

Answers – Quiz 64

316. Always crying out and cutting himself with stones. (Mark 5:5)
317. The beloved Gaius, (3 John 1:1)
318. The disciples (Acts 9:25)
319. They feared exceedingly, (Mark4:41)
320. He was asleep in the hind part of the boat (Mark 4:38)

Answers – Quiz 65

321. Many insubordinate, both idle talkers and deceivers, especially those of the circumcision (Titus 1:10-11)
322. Silvanus, and Timothy, (Both 1 & 2 Thessalonians 1:1)
323. As sheep under wolves (Matthew 10:16)
324. Decapolis (Mark 5:20)
325. Paul, Silas, Barnabas (Mark 5:18)

Answers – Quiz 66

326. An angel of the Lord instructed his parents so, because Herod commanded babies to be killed (Matthew 2:13)
327. Someone from the house of Chloe (1 Corinthians 1:11)
328. Silas (Acts 15:22)
329. A spirit of divination (Acts 16:16)
330. Two years (Acts 19:9-10)

Answers – Quiz 67

331. The return of Christ (James 5:7)
332. Pergamos (Revelation 2:12)
333. 277,915.
334. John the Baptist (Luke 7:28)
335. She touched the hem of his garment (Matthew 9:20)

Answers – Quiz 68

336. Jesus went with him and raised his daughter from the dead (Luke 8"41-55)
337. "And" 51,714 (KJV) 38,205 (NKJV) 26,532 (ISV)
338. Fourteen years (Galatians 2:1)
339. Jannes and Jambres (2 Timothy 3:8)
340. Barnabas (Acts 9:27)

Answers – Quiz 69

341. They killed him and cast him out (Mark 12:8)
342. For since the creation of the world His invisible attributes are clearly seen, being understood by the things that are made, even His eternal power and Godhead, so that they are without excuse, 1:21 because, although they knew God, they did not glorify Him as God, nor were thankful, but became futile in their thoughts, and their foolish hearts were darkened.
343. Epaphras (Filemon 1:23)
344. They asked him to go away (Mark 5:17)
345. Acts

Answers – Quiz 70

346. Luke (Acts 1:1)
347. Weighty and powerful (2 Corinthians 10:10)
348. "If any man desires to be first,…." "the same shall be last of all, and servant of all." (Mark 9:35)
349. Acts of the Apostles
350. "The baptism of John—where was it from? From heaven or from men?" (Matthew 21:25)

Answers – Quiz 71

351. An evil spirit (Acts 19:15)
352. They marveled (Mark.12:17)
353. Tertius (Romans 16:22)
354. Joel and David (Acts 2:16, 25)
355. On the island of Patmos. (Revelation 1:9-10)

Answers – Quiz 72

356. The answer of a good conscience toward God (1 Peter 3:21)
357. Was said by which people? They who asked for Jesus to be crucified (Matthew 27:25)
358. Mark 9:23
359. Quirinius (Luke 2:3)
360. Ungodly men (Jude 1:4)

Answers – Quiz 73

361. He wanted to apprehend Paul (2 Corinthians 11:32)
362. Judas Iscariot (Matthew 26:14-15)
363. With Troas, at Carpus (2 Timothy 4:13)
364. Joseph (Genesis 39:20) Samson (Judges 16:21) and Paul (Acts 16:24)
365. Artemas or Tychicus (Titus 3:12)

Answers – Quiz 74

366. James (Jude 1:1)
367. Satan (1 Thessalonians 2:18)
368. John (Revelation 1:4)
369. Herod Antipas (Mark 6:27)
370. Peter (both 1 & 2 Peter 1:1)

Answers – Quiz 75

371. James and John (Matthew 4:21)
372. John
373. Diana (Acts 19:24-28)
374. Garden of Gethsemane (Mark 14:32, 46)
375. Peter (Matthew 17:27)

Answers – Quiz 76

376. Philippi (Acts 16:11, 23)
377. Agrippa to Paul (Acts 26:28)
378. Zenas (Titus 3:13)
379. Pearls (Revelation 21:21)
380. He was the first martyr for the Gospel of Jesus Christ. (Acts 7:59)

Answers – Quiz 77

381. Tychicus (Ephesians 6:21)
382. Matthew's appointment as disciple (Matthew 9:9)
383. Matthew
384. (God our Saviour) "who desires all men to be saved and to come to the knowledge of the truth."
385. The Thessalonians (2 Thessalonians 1:4)

Answers – Quiz 78

386. Thomas (John 20:25)
387. Shield (Ephesians 6:16)
388. She had a young daughter who had an evil spirit, and she wanted Jesus to heal her (Mark 7:24-26)
389. Love (1 Corinthians 13)
390. They came to life and reigned with Christ for a thousand years (Revelation 20:4)

Extra-Biblical TRIVIA

Quiz 1

1. What is the name of the country of Mother Teresa's birth?
2. When was the Bible's first English translation finished?
3. What city do Jews, Christians and Muslims all consider to be holy?
4. What do you call a Catholic minister?
5. What do we call the day on which Christ was resurrected?

Quiz 2

6. What do we call someone who believes there is no God?
7. The Bible is the book with the largest amount of copies sold. True or false?
8. What is the meaning of the word "Eve?"
9. Who was the last ruler to cleanse the feet of the needy on Maundy Thursday, in meekness and commemoration of when Jesus cleansed the feet of the disciples?
10. Out of 266 popes, how many met a brutal end?

Quiz 3

11. What nautical item is popularly thought to be a mark of the Camino de Santiago?
12. Where are brides meant to walk to in the church, according to widespread opinion?
13. What is the term for a person who thinks that the reality of God cannot be proven?
14. What is the meaning of the word "gospel"?
15. Where does the Santiago de Compostela, or Original Way, established in the 9th century, begin?

Quiz 4

16. What Food of the Gods is believed to make people immortal?
17. The first complete Bible that was produced in America, was written in which language?
18. How many Spanish popes have there been?
19. Which hymn has the following words: "I fear no foe, with Thee at hand to bless, Ills have no weight and tears no bitterness."
20. Which day on the calendar is known as St James' day?

Quiz 5

21. "We are more popular than Jesus now." Who made people very mad with these words?
22. What is Camino de Santiago, the popular mission route, called in English?
23. When was the first edition of the Bible printed through use of movable type?
24. What word describes the thought that Jesus is not God?
25. The Vulgate Bible was translated by which Saint?

Quiz 6

26. What are Bible Beans, as advertised on Radio Luxemburg in the 1930s?
27. Which person was known as the Scourge of God?
28. Which hymn starts with these words?
29. Who is quoted as saying: "There is nothing in the bible that says I must wear rags."?
30. What is the study of final things such as death, judgement, and the apocalypse known as, in theology?

Quiz 7

31. How far would you need to go by bike on the Pilgrimage, to be awarded a certificate of accomplishment?
32. Which singer called his Top Ten Album of 1977, Exodus?
33. What, in the Christian church, occurs 49 days before Whitsunday and 40 days after Shrove Tuesday?
34. What day is the first day of Lent?
35. What is the name for the incense burner that is often swung around on a set of chains?

Quiz 8

36. Which saint is believed to have introduced Christianity in India?
37. Which is the largest religion in the world in terms of the number of believers?
38. St. Boniface is the Patron Saint of what European country?
39. Salvador Dali painted a painting called "The Ascension of Christ." What feature of Christ's body is most prominent in this painting?
40. What did Thomas Jefferson do that resulted in many people proclaiming him an infidel?

Quiz 9

41. What is the name of the Vatican's Army?
42. Who is the Patron Saint of Young Virgins?
43. Which grouping of three Christian denominations includes only Protestant denominations?
44. What was the title of the book, which was essentially a rewrite of the Bible, that removed Jesus' divinity from the story?
45. When was Christmas first celebrated?

Quiz 10

46. Who is the Patron Saint of shoe-makers whose feast day is celebrated on the 25th October?
47. Which letters denote Jesus Nazareth King of the Jews?
48. What is the tall cross or crucifix (made tall by being attached to a pole) known as?
49. The Crusaded spanned through which centuries?
50. Which movement within the Christian Church is working towards its eventual reunification?

Quiz 11

51. In which language Jesus preached?
52. Most Popes have been Italian. Which country has the 2nd highest number of Popes?
53. St. Angela of Foligno, who lived from c.1248 to 1309, was a Christian mystic and spiritual writer who became known by what title?
54. Which is the most Christian state in America?
55. What European city first heard Christian preaching?

Quiz 12

56. In which year Christianity is believed to have introduced in India?
57. Which boys name means: "he who resembles God"?
58. Who is the patron saint of lost or stolen articles?
59. What are the 3 branches of Christianity?
60. Which is the mother of religion of Christianity and Islam?

Quiz 13

61. The members of which Christian sect have no ministers or priests and gather for worship in a Meeting House?
62. Who would you expect to find in Castle Gondolofo?
63. Who was the first person born in the Americas to be canonized?
64. Who was the founder of the Franciscan order and patron saint of animals and ecology?
65. What colourful festival is celebrated on and named after Shrove Tuesday, the day before the Lenten fast?

Quiz 14

66. Who is the Patron Saint of children?
67. In how many languages has the Bible been fully translated?
68. Which Christian religious order was founded by Ignatius of Loyola?
69. What other name is the Martin Luther's Disputation on the Power and Efficacy of Indulgences known as?
70. This organization was founded by salesmen who wanted to find Bibles when on the road. Who are they?

Quiz 15

71. In a Church or a Cathedral you would find a 'reredos' and what is it?
72. What state was the first to adopt *Christianity* as its national religion?
73. Which Saint is considered the first Christian martyr, stoned to death in approximately 34 A.D.?
74. Which members of the Christian Church believe that Christ will make a second appearance on the Earth?
75. Which country has the largest Christian population?

76. That is the name of the established Church of Scotland which follows a Calvinistic doctrine?
77. Which group of three entities is typically described as making up the Christian Trinity?
78. When did Andrew Lloyd Webber's Jesus Christ Superstar first opened in Broadway?
79. What was the name of the prophet on whose book Joseph Smith founded The Church of Jesus Christ of Latter-day Saints?
80. Which word is also used to refer to the second coming of Christ?

Quiz 17

81. Which monarchs, perhaps better known for their association with a Genoese explorer in 1492, established the Spanish Inquisition in 1478?
82. Who were the first bishops of the Methodist Episcopal Church?
83. According to popular belief, how did Pope Adriano IV die?
84. When is Saint Patrick's day celebrated?
85. Who were the first bishops of the Methodist Episcopal Church?

Quiz 18

86. To which religious order does Pope Francis belong to?
87. Which American preacher is most often associated with the First Great Awakening (circa 1730-1755)?
88. Who starred in the 1988 movie 'The Mission'?
89. How many US presidents were catholic?
90. What is the liturgical colour most often associated with Ascension Day in the Western Church?

Quiz 19

91. How long did John Paul I's pontificate last?
92. Which Christian communion uses The Book of Common Prayer?
93. Who sang 'What if God was one of us?
94. What is the name of the monophonic, or unison, liturgical music of the Roman Catholic Church, used to accompany the text of the mass and the canonical hours, or divine office?
95. When was the Act of Supremacy, which declared that Henry was the "Supreme Head on earth of the Church of England", pass?

Quiz 20

96. How did Joan of Arc die?
97. Who directed the 1988 film 'The Last Temptation of Christ'?
98. In which century was the Spanish Inquisition abolished?

Extra-Biblical

TRIVIA

<u>Answers</u>

Answers – Quiz 1

1.   She was born in Skopje, in the Republic of Macedonia.
2.   During the 1380's, handwritten, by John Wycliffe.
3.   Jerusalem.
4.   A priest
5.   Easter Sunday.

Answers – Quiz 2

6.   An atheist.
7.   True
8.   Hebrew name is "Chavvâh", meaning "Lifegiver" (Strong's Hebrew & Greek Dictionary)
9.   James II
10. 33 according to tradition.

Answers – Quiz 3

11. Scallop shell
12. The nave of the church
13. Agnostic
14. Good news; glad tiding.
15. Oviedo

Answers – Quiz 4

16. Ambrosia
17. Algonquin Indian
18. Two–Pope Alexander VI and Pope Callixtus III
19. "Abide with me."
20. 25th July

Answers – Quiz 5

21. John Lennon
22. The Way of St. James (or St. James Path)
23. 1455
24. Arianism
25. Jerome

Answers – Quiz 6

26. Laxatives
27. Attila the Hun
28. "O Lord, my God, when I in awesome wonder consider all the world Thy hands have made..." How great thou art.
29. Billy Graham
30. Eschatology

Answers – Quiz 7

31. 200 km
32. Bob Marley
33. Easter
34. Ash Wednesday
35. Thurible

Answers – Quiz 8

36. Saint Thomas.
37. Christianity
38. Germany
39. His feet
40. He claimed Jesus was not the son of God

Answers – Quiz 9

41. The Swiss Guard.
42. St Agnes
43. Methodism, Presbyterianism, Lutheranism
44. The Life and Morals of Jesus of Nazareth
45. 336 AD

Answers – Quiz 10

46. Saint Crispin.
47. INRI
48. Processional cross
49. 11th, 12th and 13th centuries.
50. Ecumenical movement.

Answers – Quiz 11

51. In Aramaic language.
52. France
53. Mistress of Theologians
54. Alabama
55. Philippi.

Answers – Quiz 12

56. About A.D. 50.
57. Michael
58. Anthony of Padua
59. Orthodox, Catholic, Protestant.
60. Judaism, the religion of the Jews.

Answers – Quiz 13

61. Quakers (Society of Friends).
62. St. Rose of Lima
63. The Pope
64. Francis of Assisi
65. Mardi Gras.

Answers – Quiz 14

66. Saint Nicholas.
67. 698
68. Jesuits
69. Ninety-five theses.
70. The Gideons

Answers – Quiz 15

71. An ornamental screen at the back of the altar or communion table.
72. Kingdom of Armenia
73. Stephen
74. Adventists.
75. USA

Answers – Quiz 16

76. Presbyterianism.
77. Father, Son, Holy Spirit
78. 1971
79. Mormon.
80. Parousia

Answers – Quiz 17

81. Ferdinand II of Aragon and Isabella I of Castile
82. Thomas Coke and Francis Asbury
83. He choked on a fly in his wine
84. March 17th
85. Thomas Coke and Francis Asbury

Answers – Quiz 18

86. Society of Jesus
87. Jonathan Edwards
88. Robert de Niro
89. 1, John F. Kennedy
90. White

Answers – Quiz 19

91. 33 days
92. The Anglican
93. Joan Osborne
94. Gregorian chant
95. 1534.

Answers – Quiz 20

96. Execution by burning
97. Martin Scorsese
98. 19th century

Printed in Great Britain
by Amazon

80943093R00079